CULTURE SMART!

TURKEY

THE ESSENTIAL GUIDE TO CUSTOMS & CULTURE

CHARLOTTE McPHERSON

KUPERARD

"The real voyage of discovery consists not in seeking new landscapes, but in having new eyes."

Adapted from Marcel Proust, *Remembrance of Things Past.*

ISBN 978 1 78702 3185
British Library Cataloguing in Publication Data
A CIP catalogue entry for this book is available
from the British Library

First published in Great Britain
by Kuperard, an imprint of Bravo Ltd
59 Hutton Grove, London N12 8DS
Tel: +44 (0) 20 8446 2440
www.culturesmart.co.uk
Inquiries: publicity@kuperard.co.uk

Design Bobby Birchall
Printed in Turkey by Elma Basim

The Culture Smart! series is continuing to expand.
All Culture Smart! guides are available as e-books, and many
as audio books. For further information and latest titles visit
www.culturesmart.co.uk

CHARLOTTE McPHERSON is an American who has lived in Turkey since 1979. For her graduate studies at Indiana University she specialized in Uralic Altaic languages and history. She has an MA in Anthropology, and during the 1980s she conducted extensive research in Turkey and Central Asia among Turkic-speaking peoples. She has lectured in Social Anthropology at Mimar Sinan University, Istanbul, and has served as Vice President of the Turkish-American University Cultural Association. A regular columnist for a popular English-language newspaper for ten years, today Charlotte lives in Istanbul where she owned and managed a major English-language bookstore, Greenhouse, for two decades.

CONTENTS

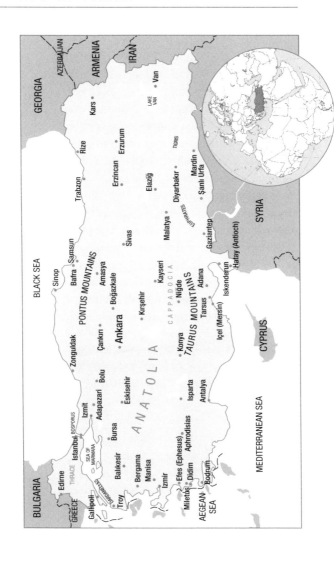

INTRODUCTION

Turkey has always attracted travelers. Over the centuries the landmass of Asia Minor, heart of the great multicultural Ottoman Empire and now the modern Republic of Turkey, experienced waves of migrations in which one civilization displaced another, leaving a unique and glorious cultural heritage. Its heroic landscapes, magnificent ruins, miles of stunning beaches, and legendary hospitality continue to draw visitors to its shores.

At first glance, Turkey seems Westernized and modern in many ways—but this appearance is misleading. It is a land of contrasts, a heady mixture of Oriental mystery and romance and ultramodern city life, deep-rooted religious faith and determined secularism, a fierce sense of national pride and openness to foreign ideas. Turkish culture is a distinctive blend of European and Middle Eastern ways of life.

One remarkable man was responsible for creating modern Turkey. In 1923 Mustafa Kemal (known as Atatürk, "the Father of the Turks") took control and transformed the country from an absolute feudal monarchy to today's secular, democratic Muslim state. Tales of this one-man revolution abound, and he is genuinely revered. His image is still everywhere, and his legacy a source of national pride. Patriotism is a Turkish virtue. However, in recent years, it appears that religious conservatives perceive the secularism and nationalism of the Kemalist establishment as oppressive doctrines; the Islamic headscarf controversy that began in the 1980s is an example of this tension.

The Turkish people are very much their own center of gravity, and for the unwary visitor there are pitfalls to avoid as well as great riches to be found. *Culture Smart! Turkey* aims to help you understand the paradoxes of Turkish life. It outlines the complex history of Anatolia, and particularly the formative years after the First World War. It provides key insights into Turkish values and attitudes, describes important customs and traditions, and reveals what life is like for the Turks at home, at work, and at play. It offers practical tips and information about what to expect and how to behave in different situations.

This fascinating and important country is not only the cradle of European and Islamic cultures: it offers opportunities for enjoyable exploration, new friendships, academic studies, and business development. The Turks are very hospitable, open, and pleased to meet foreigners. If you show an interest in their culture and respect for their point of view, they will repay your effort many times over.

Official Name	Turkiye Cumhuriyeti (Republic of Turkey)	Turkey is a member of NATO, the Council of Europe, and an associate member of the European Union.
Capital City	Ankara	Population approx. 5.7 million
Main Cities	Istanbul. Officially the population is 15.8 million; unofficially between 16 and 18 million.	Other cities: Izmir, Bursa, Adana, Gaziantep, Konya, Antalya, Diyarbakır, Mersin
Population	84.6 million approx.	
Area	301,382 sq. miles (780,580 sq. km) 97% in Asia and 3% in Europe	
Climate	Varies considerably. The Black Sea coast is mild with a lot of rain. Middle and eastern Anatolia have hot, dry summers and cold winters. A typical Mediterranean climate is common along the Aegean and Mediterranean Seas.	
Language	Turkish, written in the Latin script	Minority languages incl. Kurdish, Arabic, Armenian, Greek
Religion	Turkey is a secular republic: 99.8% of people are Muslim.	Other religions: Christianity and Judaism

Government	Secular democratic republic	A system of executive presidency was introduced in 2017 under which the president is now both head of state and head of govt., and is voted in directly by the electorate every 5 years.
Currency	Turkish Lira (TRY)	
Economy	Main exports include: cars and vehicle parts, machinery including computers, gold, iron, and steel, crude and refined petroleum, and hand-woven rugs.	Main imports include: Gold, refined petroleum, cars and vehicle parts, scrap iron, synthetic yarn, and sunflower seeds.
Media	TRT is the national TV and radio network. There are numerous local and commercial satellite stations.	There are numerous private radio stations. Various newspapers and magazines in Turkish, English, and other languages are available.
Electricity	220 volts (50 Hz)	2-pronged plugs used
Internet Domain	.tr	
Telephone	Turkey's country code is +90.	To dial out of Turkey, dial 00 and then the country code.
Time Zone	GMT + 3 hours	

CHAPTER ONE

LAND & PEOPLE

GEOGRAPHICAL SNAPSHOT

Situated at the southeastern corner of Europe, Turkey straddles the straits that divide Europe and Asia—the Dardanelles, the Sea of Marmara, and the Bosporus. Three percent of its landmass lies in Europe, giving it borders with Greece and Bulgaria, while 97 percent lies in Asia. The enormous Asian part, known as Anatolia, shares borders on the east and south with Georgia, Armenia, Azerbaijan, Iran, Iraq, and Syria. The country is bounded on three sides by water: the Aegean Sea to the west, the Mediterranean to the south, and the Black Sea to the north.

European Turkey is the most densely populated part of the country. In Anatolia, the population is densest in the west, in urban centers such as Istanbul, Bursa, Izmir, and Izmit, and decreases steadily toward the east. In the interior the population is concentrated along the paths of rivers and in towns such as Ankara,

Soumela Monastery at Karadağ, in the Pontus Mountain range.

Eskişehir, Konya, Erzurum, Malatya, and Kayseri.
Most of the Central Anatolian Highlands consist of
undulating hills and broad, high plateaus from which
mountains occasionally rise. The population of the
south coast is massed on the fertile plains of Antalya
and Adana, as well as in the province of Hatay, with its
port of Iskenderun. As in other countries around the
world, there is a steady trend of people moving into
the cities from rural areas, though in the past decade,
the Turkish government has tried to reduce the flow
of migration to major urban centers by investing in
historic preservation, urban revitalization, community
development, high-speed train links, and sustainable
tourism in peripheral towns and cities.

Enclosing the Central Anatolian Highlands are two
great mountain ranges: the Pontus Mountains in the

Mount Ararat as seen from the eastern town of Doğubeyazıt.

north, and the Taurus range to the south. The most famous mountain is Mount Ararat in the east, where Noah's Ark is reputed to have come to rest. Turkey is rich in water, the lifeblood of the Middle East. The most important rivers of the region, the Tigris and the Euphrates, each have their source here.

CLIMATE

Turkey's latitude would lead one to expect a broadly temperate or Mediterranean climate. Owing to its topography, however, the country's climate varies according to region. Turks claim that all four seasons can be experienced in any one day, albeit in different parts of the country.

The Black Sea coast has a predominantly mild summer and winter. It is the area with the heaviest rainfall (pack an umbrella for a trip here!) and is famous for its tea plantations.

The Mediterranean and Aegean coasts have a typical Mediterranean climate, with long, hot, dry summers and mild winters.

The Marmara coast is a climatic transitional zone between the first two. It is hot, but does not have such dry summers. The winters are cool, with occasional frosts and outbreaks of snow.

Central Anatolia has a markedly continental climate, with hot summers around 86°F (30°C), and bitterly cold, snowy winters, sometimes down to -22°F (-30°C). There can also be large swings in temperature between day and night throughout the year.

A BRIEF HISTORY

When the Turks entered Anatolia in the eleventh century, they encountered a cosmopolitan civilization that was itself the product of many earlier traditions. Turkish tolerance, pluralism, and openness to new ideas led to a cultural exchange that resulted in an extraordinary flowering of Islamic humanism. They created a great inclusive empire that transformed the societies they absorbed and lasted nearly a thousand years. Turks are proud not only of their own remarkable achievements, but of the fact that the ancient civilizations of their homeland are part of the inheritance of mankind.

Early Anatolian Civilizations

Sophisticated Neolithic (8000–5000 BCE) settlements with religious shrines, decorated houses, and pottery dating to the seventh and sixth millennia BCE have been found at Hacilar and Çatalhöyük in central Anatolia.

In the Bronze Age (3000–2000 BCE) two remarkable civilizations arose: the Mesopotamian-influenced Hatti in central and southeastern Anatolia, and the Mycenean settlement of Troy in northwestern Anatolia.

At the beginning of the second millennium BCE, an Indo-European people, the Hittites, entered Anatolia via the Caucasus and gradually absorbed the Hatti. Their powerful empire, with its capital at Hattusas (Boghazkoi), vied with Egypt for domination of the Near East in the thirteenth century BCE.

A rare Hittite artifact, a silver fist-shaped drinking cup, dated to the fourteenth century BCE.

Roughly contemporary with the Hittites were the Mitani, who spoke Hurrian, in eastern Anatolia, and the civilization of Troy VI, the great walled Ilion of Homer's Iliad that commanded the Hellespont (the Dardanelles).

Around 1200 BCE, invasions by Indo-European tribes from Thrace utterly destroyed Troy and Hattusas, and a dark age followed. By the Iron Age (c. 1000 BCE) Anatolia was divided into numerous principalities. They included the Late Hittites in southeastern Anatolia, the Urartians in the region of Lake Van, the Phrygians in central and southeastern Anatolia, the Lydians, Carians, and Lycians in the west and southwest, and, on the western coastal fringe, the Ionians.

The Phrygians became a major power and established their capital at Gordion, between Ankara and Eskişehir. Monuments of the last Phrygian king, Midas (c. 715 BCE), still remain around Eskişehir.

The Lydian kingdom (750–300 BCE) was the first to invent a system of coinage, which revolutionized commerce. Sardis, the capital, was reputedly the richest city in the ancient world because of its gold mines. The wealth and might of its last king, Croesus, became proverbial.

Ionian Greeks began colonizing the western coast of Anatolia in around 1050 BCE. Their city-states included Miletus and Ephesus. In their most brilliant period, the sixth century BCE, they gave the world philosophy and free scientific thought and became the center of poetry and the arts.

After the defeat of Croesus of Lydia by Cyrus the Great of Persia in 546 BCE, Anatolia came under Persian rule. For the first time in its history it served as a bridge between Asia and Europe—the Royal Road built by the Persians joined Iran to the Aegean coast.

The Hellenistic Age (333–30 BCE)

Alexander the Great's victory over the Persians at the Battle of Issus in 333 BCE restored the independence of Anatolia's Hellenistic cities, which regained their cultural supremacy. After Alexander's death the western Anatolian kingdom of Pergamum rivaled Alexandria in cultural, scientific, and artistic achievement.

A first century mosaic depicting Alexander the Great at the Battle of Issus.

The Roman Age (30 BCE–395 CE)

Through a combination of inheritance, conquest, and alliances, Rome began to establish provinces in Anatolia from the second century BCE: Pergamum, Bithynia and Pontus, Galatia, Pisidia, Cilicia, and Cappadocia. Julius Caesar reportedly uttered the words "I came, I saw, I conquered" when announcing his military victory at Zela, near modern-day Tokat, in 47 BCE. Anatolia prospered within the Roman Empire and by the second century CE, Anatolia's cities rivaled Rome itself.

Byzantine Civilization (330–1453 CE)

Anatolia was the cradle of Christianity: Saint Paul was born in Tarsus in Cilicia. Many of his missionary journeys in the first century CE were to Anatolian

cities—Ephesus, Konya, Troas, Miletus, Colossae. Indeed, followers of Christ were first called "Christians" in Antioch (Antakya) and the Seven Churches of the Book of Revelation were all in western Anatolia. Many of Paul's epistles, and those of Peter, were written to believers in Anatolia. In 325 CE the first general council of the Church met in

A mural depicting Emperor Constantine presenting the Hagia Sophia.

Nicea (Iznik), where it proclaimed the doctrine of the Trinity and established the Nicene Creed.

In 330 CE Constantine the Great made the ancient city of Byzantium the eastern capital of the Roman Empire and renamed it Constantinople. After the fall of Rome in the fifth century, the eastern Empire—which continued to consider itself Roman—presided over a civilization that lasted a thousand years, spanned the Middle Ages, and played a vital role in the interchange of ideas between East and West. Constantinople became one of the most important intellectual and cultural centers in the world.

The Arrival of the Turks

The ancestors of the modern Turks were nomadic tribesmen who lived on the steppes of Inner Asia in the sixth century CE. Over the next thousand years, after a series of conquests, different Turkic clans created a succession of multicultural, polyethnic empires that stretched from China to the Mediterranean. The Oghuz Turks moved west to Transoxiana (roughly modern-day Uzbekistan and southwest Kazakhstan), where they settled and embraced Islam, before migrating south to Iran. There they founded the Great Seljuk State, which created an inclusive Turkic, Arab, and Persian culture. Waves of breakaway tribes from the Oghuz confederation started entering Anatolia, where each would establish a kingdom, only to fall to the next Turkic group to come their way.

By 1000 CE the Byzantine Empire was fading away. The seat of the Empire, Constantinople, was on the

European shore of the Bosporus. The last successful Emperor, Basil II (976–1025 CE), was succeeded by weak rulers who failed to maintain the city's defenses.

In the eleventh century, the Caliph of Baghdad, the supreme religious leader of Islam, recruited Seljuk mercenaries to help him maintain his position. As a result, their leader, Tughrul, was made Sultan of Sunni Islam. The Seljuks assumed control of Baghdad, and soon their empire covered most of modern Turkey, Iraq, and Iran.

In 1071 CE the Byzantine army of Emperor Romanus IV Diogenes was utterly defeated by the Seljuk Turks at Manzikert, near Lake Van in the east. Six years later the Seljuks founded a new state in Rum, which is what the Muslims called the Eastern Roman Empire.

The Seljuk Sultanate

Following a major defeat during the First Crusade in 1097 CE, the Rum Seljuks set up their capital at Konya, formerly Iconium, in central southern Anatolia. This city stood at a crossroads and had long served as a conduit for the ideas and influences of nations of diverse ethnicity, language, and culture. There the Seljuks presided over a cultural renaissance, the building of magnificent mosques, academies, and centers of trade.

Ruins and ancient mosques testify to the splendor of Seljuk architecture and the period is famous for developing the use of brickwork, which enabled buildings to be decorated with reliefs. The Seljuks also took full advantage of the strong sunlight to create an elaborate interplay of light and shade, with the use of large portals, processional courtyards, vivid color, and intricate masonry. Their literature includes the mystical works of the great Sufi poets Rumi and Yunus Emre.

In the twelfth century CE the Byzantine Empire was shrinking, but the Seljuks were also in trouble, under pressure from Crusaders in the west and the Mongols in the east. Invasions and civil war gradually brought the Seljuk Empire to collapse in 1261 CE.

The Rise of the Ottomans

As a result of the Mongol ascendancy in Iran, Asia Minor experienced a fresh influx of displaced Oghuz Turkic tribes in the thirteenth century. The Ottoman Turks, named after their leader Osman I (1270–1326), emerged as a local power on the Byzantine-Seljuk frontier in northwestern Anatolia.

In the late 1200s, Osman established the Janissaries as an elite fighting force to expand his kingdom and by 1304 the Ottomans occupied the entire Asian side of the Sea of Marmara. Bursa became their capital in 1326 and in 1350 they crossed the Dardenelles. The capital was later moved to Edirne (old Adrianapolis) in Western Thrace in 1361, and from there the Ottomans

An illustration of Sultan Osman I, founder of the Ottoman dynasty.

began to penetrate the Balkans. Strategically positioned, practically encircling Constantinople, they slowly sapped the remaining power of the Byzantine emperors.

The clash of empires was also one of religion. Byzantium was the Holy Eastern Roman Empire. The Ottoman state was Muslim; to the political title of Sultan, the Ottoman rulers would later add the spiritual title of Caliph when Mameluke Cairo was added to their lands in 1517. Despite this, economic and social ties developed between Byzantium and Anatolia, particularly after the sack of Orthodox Constantinople by the Latin Crusaders in 1204.

Osman's grandson, Murad I, crushed a Christian coalition at Kosovo in 1389, gaining Serbia and the Balkans. The Byzantine Emperor was forced to acknowledge the Sultan as his overlord. Murad's successor, Beyazit I, defeated the last great crusade, led by Sigismund of Hungary, at Nicopolis in 1396. He then laid siege to Constantinople in 1397.

A new front opened up against the Ottomans in the east, however, when the Mongol threat resurfaced. Under the leadership of the Turco-Mongol conqueror Timur (Tamerlane), they defeated the Ottomans in a great battle on a plain near Ankara in 1402, capturing Beyazit and forcing him to raise the siege of Constantinople. This temporarily eased the pressure on the Byzantine Empire. However, the Tartars plundered Anatolia and moved on; their aim was to vanquish their enemies, not to expand to the west.

After internecine fighting among the sons of Beyazit, Murad II recovered the lost Ottoman lands and expanded their territory in southeastern Europe, paving the way for a fresh assault on Constantinople.

The Fall of Constantinople

Murad's successor, Mehmet II (1415–81), resolved to capture Constantinople for Islam. Although by now a weakened vassal state, Constantinople was home to Venetian and Genoese fleets that could cut the Turkish realm in two. In 1452, in just four months, Mehmet II built the fortress of Rumeli Hisar on the European side of the Bosporus north of Constantinople, thus closing the Bosporus to the city. The city walls were strong and

Mehmet II and his soldiers entering Constantinople, by nineteenth century Italian painter Fausto Zonaro.

fiercely defended, and access to the Golden Horn was barred by a great chain that stretched from shore to shore. Mehmet's masterstroke was to construct a huge causeway that enabled his army to haul their boats overland from the shore of the Bosporus into the Golden Horn, thus launching a naval attack from the north. The city walls were breached on May 29, 1453, and one glorious chapter in history came to a bloody end, to be succeeded by another.

This victory confirmed the Ottoman's European Empire. Mehmet II became known as Mehmet the Conqueror. He made Constantinople his capital and renamed it Istanbul. In the years that followed he built palaces, markets, mosques, and religious colleges. An intellectual steeped in Western classical culture—he spoke six languages, including Latin and Greek— Mehmet employed Greek and Italian advisers, and commissioned works by Italian artists.

The Ottoman Empire

The Empire attained its greatest glory in the reign of Süleyman the Magnificent (1520–66). This was a golden age in which glorious palaces and mosques were built, including the Sülemaniye Mosque in Istanbul, designed by Süleyman's chief architect, Sinan. Süleyman is known to the Turks as Kanuni, "the lawgiver," and there were great advances in the process of government under him.

During the sixteenth and seventeenth centuries, the Ottoman Empire grew by conquest, until it spread across North Africa, Arabia, Iraq, the Black Sea, and Ukraine, and into Europe as far as Hungary. Its advance was famously halted at the gates of Vienna in 1683, though not before the Ottomans had left their wonderful coffee behind.

Portrait of Süleyman the Magnificent by Titian, circa 1530.

Pressed back by Russian and Austrian armies, the Ottoman Empire experienced a decline in governance in the eighteenth century and neglected its foreign affairs. In the nineteenth century, it began to lose territories in the Aegean, the Balkans, North Africa, and Arabia.

The Crimean War

A brief interlude in this period of decline was the Crimean War. Regarded by Britain as a bulwark against Russian expansionism, the Ottoman Empire fought with Britain and France against the Russians in the Crimean Peninsula in 1854–56. This war was the setting for Florence Nightingale's famous hospital at Scutari (Üsküdar). In the end Russia was vanquished. The Treaty of Paris declared the Black Sea neutral, closed it to all warships, and prohibited fortifications and the presence of armaments on its shores. The independence of Turkey was affirmed and Russian influence in the area received a setback. Despite this settlement, Turkish power continued to wane as the European powers fomented separatism among its subjects, particularly in the Balkans.

The Loss of the Balkans

Confronted by the loss of Ottoman power and turmoil in the Balkans, the young Sultan Abdülhamid II, to appease his critics, presented a liberal constitution to a conference called by the European powers in Istanbul in 1876. The following year he retracted it and took absolute control. War broke out again in the Balkans, and Russia, which joined the insurgents, was victorious. By the terms of the Treaty of San Stefano (1878) the Ottoman Empire lost most of its European possessions. Its decline was so pronounced that by the end of the century it was called "the sick man of Europe."

At home, Abdülhamid's failed promises and misgovernment led to rising discontent and pressure for change. In 1908 the group of reformers known as the "Young Turks" forced him to restore the constitution of 1876. He was deposed by a unanimous vote of parliament in 1909 and succeeded by his brother Muhammad V. From then until the outbreak of the First World War power was shared uneasily between the Sultan and the leaders of the Young Turks. In 1911–12, Tripoli (Libya) was lost to Italy. The Balkan War of 1912–13 with Greece, Serbia, and Bulgaria saw Ottoman territory in Europe reduced to an area around Adrianople and Constantinople. Because of its close economic and political links with Germany, the Ottoman Empire entered the First World War on the Kaiser's side.

The End of Empire: The Treaty of Sèvres

With the defeat of Germany in 1918 came humiliation for its Turkish ally. The Ottoman Empire was dissolved by the crushing terms of the Treaty of Sèvres, signed in 1920 with the victorious Allies (excluding Russia and the USA). The regional map was redrawn: Turkey renounced sovereignty over Mesopotamia (Iraq) and Palestine (including Transjordan), which became British mandates; Syria and Lebanon, which became French mandates; and the kingdom of Hejaz (meaning the loss of Mecca).

Perhaps the most controversial terms were those that compelled Turkey to allow Armenia to become a separate republic under international guarantees, and to see Smyrna (now Izmir) and its environs put under an interim Greek administration, with the final outcome to be decided by a vote for national self-determination by the local electorate.

In Europe, Turkey ceded parts of Eastern Thrace and certain Aegean islands to Greece, and the Dodecanese and Rhodes to Italy, retaining only Istanbul and its environs, including the neutralized and internationalized zone of the Straits. No part of Turkey was left fully independent. Turkey also had to pay reparations, enabling the Allies to tighten their control over the economy. The Treaty of Sèvres thus spelled the end of the Ottoman Empire, placed its lands in the hands of the Allies, and sparked the patriotic fire that drove Atatürk to fight for an independent Turkish nation.

Atatürk

It is worth pausing to consider the continuing impact of these events on the present day. As a visitor to Turkey you will soon recognize the face of Mustafa Kemal Atatürk, from pictures on the walls of shops, workplaces, and government buildings, and from his statue in every public square. But you will not see cartoons of him, or hear a joke about him. Atatürk

(1881–1938) is revered as a visionary whose ideas changed the nation, who broke the power of the Sultan, and who created the modern Republic. Defamation of his person or character by any means is regarded as defamation of "Turkishness" and is against the law.

Mustafa Kemal (the family name Atatürk was later conferred on him by

Mustafa Kemal Atatürk, 1930.

the National Assembly) was a brilliant soldier. He served as a commander in the First World War, rising to fame by repulsing the Allied assault at Gallipoli in 1915–16. This forced the Allies to retreat from European Turkey and led to the political ostracism of Winston Churchill, who had planned the campaign.

In the period between the end of the war and the announcing of the terms of the Treaty of Sèvres, the Sultan, Muhammad VI, was losing control—both to the victorious powers who were planning to carve up the Ottoman Empire and to nationalist rejection of his rule. In 1919, he sent Mustafa Kemal to crush a rebellion that had broken out in the Black Sea area around Samsun. Instead of doing this, Mustafa Kemal renounced his rank and titles and joined the insurgents. Along with a number of other military officers he established a national government at a conference in the eastern city of Erzurum, in opposition to the Sultan in Istanbul.

On April 23, 1920, Mustafa Kemal convened a National Assembly in Ankara that drew up a manifesto demanding the independence and integrity of all parts of the Ottoman Empire "inhabited by an Ottoman Muslim" majority, effectively repudiating the Treaty of Sèvres. Kemal inspired the nation to reject the postwar division of Turkey and defy the occupying British, French, and Italian forces. In 1921 the provisional government in Ankara transferred political power to the people.

It formally abolished the Ottoman Sultanate, and in 1922 the Sultan was deposed and went into exile in Europe.

The War of Independence

In 1921 Greece ordered 100,000 troops into Anatolia, ostensibly to support the Greeks of Izmir. For the new Turkish nation there was no turning back. When Atatürk launched the counteroffensive he told his soldiers to march to the Aegean, saying "I offer you the choice: freedom or death." The Greek army was defeated at Dumlupınar on August 26, and at Izmir on September 9, 1922. Izmir was destroyed. The Turkish struggle for national sovereignty lasted three years, and by its end the Turks had driven all foreign forces from their land.

These victories united the nation and restored the Turks' belief in themselves. The reconquest of Anatolia undid the Treaty of Sèvres. Mustafa Kemal made a separate treaty with the USSR and forced the Allies to negotiate a new settlement. The Treaty of Lausanne, signed in 1923, confirmed Turkey's lands in Anatolia and removed the obligation to pay reparations. The fate of minority populations was a major element. The Treaty opened the way for a large population exchange, with many hundreds of thousands of Greeks leaving Turkey and a smaller number of Turks leaving Greece, and secured the rights of minorities who stayed in Turkey.

The Turkish Republic

The Turks had moved their capital from Istanbul to undeveloped Ankara. There, on October 29, 1923, a secular nationalist republic was declared, and Mustafa Kemal was unanimously elected first President of the Republic of Turkey. The Constitution of 1924 provided for an interim period of one-party rule—that of his Republican People's Party. This allowed for a controlled transition to full democracy.

After 1923 Mustafa Kemal embarked on a sweeping program of Westernization and economic development. He drove through a series of revolutionary social and political reforms that dealt with every aspect of the life of the people. The Caliphate was abolished and Islam was disestablished. Western-style dress was introduced and the wearing of veils by women and the fez by men was banned. The Turkish language was purged of Arabic words and the alphabet changed from Arabic to Latin script. Education was secularized. Literacy programs were organized and education for women and villagers became mandatory. Polygamy was banned. The Gregorian calendar was introduced, the administration overhauled, and new legal codes introduced. The communications infrastructure, the country's finances, and agricultural and industrial methods were improved. In 1934, when the use of surnames was instituted, Mustafa Kemal chose the name Atatürk, which means "Father of the Turks."

Atatürk died at the age of fifty-seven in Dolmabahçe Palace, Istanbul, on November 10, 1938. His legacy was nothing less than the transformation of Turkey from an absolute feudal monarchy into a modern, secular, sovereign state, free from foreign interference, whose citizens enjoyed greater freedom and security than their forefathers had ever known.

Modern Turkey

Atatürk was succeeded as president by his friend and colleague Ismet Inönü. Turkey was neutral through most of the Second World War, before siding with the Allies. With the development of the Cold War, steps were taken to identify with the West. In 1946 Turkey became a charter member of the United Nations. In 1950 the first free elections were held and won by the opposition Democratic Party. Great efforts were made to liberalize the economy. In 1952 Turkey joined NATO, and in 1964 it became an associate member of the European Economic Community.

Following the example of Atatürk, the Turkish army assumed a special role as protector of the Republic's secular ideals. It stood at the ready to preserve his legacy if politicians appeared to be taking steps to reverse any of his reforms. Turkey experienced three military coups within three decades. In the late 1950s, political and economic instability caused anarchy and violence. This led to a bloodless military coup in 1960 led by General Cemal Gürsel. In 1971 strikes and student unrest led to another coup. Military rule lasted until elections were held in 1973. The years to come were full of economic and social problems. Tension between the political left and right increased. The 1970s saw a string of coalition governments. By the end of the decade political violence had reached such a level that in 1980 another military regime was imposed by General Kenan Evren.

In 1983 there was a return to civilian rule. Turgut Özal was elected as prime minister, and a new constitution restructured the country to be more in line with the West. Özal and his Motherland Party focused on economic growth and further opening up Turkey to the West. Özal's reforms narrowed the political and economic gap between Turkey and Europe; (he was later president between 1989 and 1993). In 1996 Necmettin Erbakan and his religiously conservative Welfare Party rose to power and he was prime minister for one year before the military ousted him.

After Turkey experienced a series of economic shocks in 2002, a major political power shift occurred, putting the religious conservative party Justice and Development Party (AKP) in power, a position in which they remain since. The AKP was founded in 2001; one of the founders is current President Recep Tayyip Erdoğan, who previously served as prime minister from 2003 to 2014 and mayor of Istanbul from 1994 to 1998.

President Recep Tayyip Erdoğan.

One of the key events in the early part of the AKP government's rule was the "Ergenekon" trials, which were a series of high-profile court cases that involved vast numbers of military officers and other public figures accused of being members of a shadowy "deep-state" organization that committed political assassinations and various other crimes in order to thwart the democratic process. Though opinion was divided as to the veracity of the accusations, one result of the trials, which ended in 2016, was that the power and influence of the military in Turkish politics was significantly curtailed.

The AKP has also been responsible for a major effort to bring the decades-long conflict in the Kurdish-dominated southeast to an end. Talks were underway with the Kurdish separatist, terrorist, PKK organization, and many terrorists had begun to lay down their arms. The chance for peace seemed better than it had for many years and in 2013 a ceasefire was called. However, in 2014 renewed conflict broke out stemming from a combination of domestic and regional developments, particularly in Syria and Northern Iraq, against a backdrop of growing mutual distrust.

Not all parts of Turkish society are supportive of the AKP. President Erdoğan is accused by his opponents of being authoritarian, which led to major protests across Turkey in early summer 2013. The protests were sparked by the violent eviction of environmental protesters demonstrating against development plans in Gezi Park in Istanbul. Protests and strikes spread across Turkey in support of press freedoms, freedom of expression, and freedom of assembly.

A night in recent memory that Turks will never forget is July 15, 2016, when the nation lived through a failed coup attempt. The military coup was thwarted when civilians occupied important city squares and bridges en masse, as well as by decisive military action taken by forces that remained loyal to the government. The government has since made clear that it believes that the failed coup was carried out by the Hizmet movement, who are followers of the exiled cleric Fethullah Gülen, though he has personally denied any role. The subsequent government crackdown resulted in further purges of military personnel accused of being associated with the Hizmet movement, confiscation and closures of the movement's schools, hospitals, media platforms, and publishing houses. In addition, the government enacted a state of emergency that lasted for two years. Following the coup attempt, the power of the military in Turkish politics was further curtailed.

In 2017 a constitutional referendum changed the Turkish parliamentary system to a presidential one, solidifying Erdoğan's position in public life following his election as president in 2014, after having served as prime minister from 2003.

In Turkey today, social polarization between secularists who support Atatürk's social revolution and those who believe in more traditional, conservative Islamic values is becoming more entrenched. A revealing example of the dynamic balance of power between secularists and conservatives is the magnificent

Haghia Sophia in Istanbul. First built as a church nearly 1,500 years ago, it was turned into a mosque following the Muslim conquest of the city in 1453 and later converted into a museum under Atatürk. In 2020 it was turned into a mosque once more, with prayers held on the anniversary of Mehmet the Conqueror's victory over the Byzantine Empire in Istanbul. In another example, women's Islamic headscarves are now permitted in public institutions after having been banned in the 1980s.

ATTITUDES TO HISTORY

Attitudes to history are changing in Turkey. With the foundation of the Republic, a break was made with the Ottoman past. The focus of the nation's life was moved from Ottoman Istanbul to republican Ankara. The modern period was perceived as very much better than the old. Today, with the reduction in the political and social power of secularists, there is a growing interest in all things Ottoman. Some government functions are moving back to Istanbul, and history professors are beginning to focus more on the Ottoman period than ever before. A major popular television series called "Magnificent Century" ran from 2011–2014 and focused on the life and times of Süleyman the Magnificent. More recently, the 2021 Netflix series "Rise of Empires: Ottomans" proved very popular both locally and abroad.

The Turkish People Today

Owing to a comparatively high birthrate, the Turks are a very young nation by Western standards. You will see young people everywhere, and this gives the country great dynamism and an enterprising spirit. It is astonishing to realize that only 9 percent of the Turkish population are over sixty-five!

Seventy to seventy-five percent of the population are ethnic Turks, 20 percent are Kurds, while other ethnic groups include the Laz people in the Black Sea region, Christian minorities (Armenians, Greeks, Assyrians, Suryani), and Jews.

Ever since the founding of the Republic the Turkish government has downplayed ethnic, linguistic, and religious distinctions, fearful that a divided country could become the scene of ethnic violence and civil war. Thus the 1965 census was the last one to list linguistic minorities.

The Kurds, the country's largest minority, have posed the most serious and persistent challenge to national unity. Kurdish people traditionally have lived in an area encompassing southeastern Turkey and northern Iraq. The Turkish state has always sought to minimize the differences between Turks and Kurds, often describing the latter as "mountain Turks," and its historic policies have received both the approval (for citizenship, education for all, etc.) and disapproval (for limitations on the use of the Kurdish language, etc.) of the West.

The greatest fear of the Turks is that Kurdish nationalism will result in secession, similar to that seen in the former Yugoslavia in the late twentieth century, and the breakup of their state. Many Kurds have assimilated into Turkish society and are successful businesspeople, and in recent years there have arisen prominent politicians of Kurdish origin too. However, radical Kurdish groups have taken up arms in the southeast, and perpetrated terrorist acts in Turkey's major cities. The most well-known Kurdish terror group is the PKK. A ceasefire in the late 1990s and the capture and conviction of the PKK leader Abdullah Öcalan, along with the rise of political representation through the Kurdish party HDP, brought about relative peace in the region for a period. In recent years, greater rights have been granted to minorities, such as media broadcasts in the Kurdish language.

Many Turks are suspicious that foreign powers wish to encourage Kurdish nationalism and keep a wary eye on the development of Kurdish autonomy in neighboring Iraq and Western support of Kurdish fighters in the Syrian Civil War.

A foreign visitor in Turkey would be well advised not to take sides in the debate on nationalism, or to voice opinions about certain events in Turkey's past, such as the sensitive issue of whether or not there was an Armenian massacre. All Turkish schoolchildren are taught about the Treaty of Sèvres and the attempted partition of Turkey by the Allies, and about the encouragement given to seditious and often violent minority groups at that time and as a result, Turks are sensitive to the possibility that foreign powers might still wish to destabilize the country. In short, be wary of political debate in Turkey: it can lose you friends and even result in a run-in with the authorities.

TURKISH CITIES

Istanbul

Few cities can rival Istanbul's fascinating mix of culture and history. It has been the capital of empires and for nearly 1,500 years stood at the pivot of world history. The silhouette of its skyline viewed from the Bosporus is breathtakingly beautiful, and visitors are dazzled by the richness of its cultural heritage. Istanbul is the economic powerhouse of Turkey. As real estate prices increase, there is a trend toward building taller tower blocks, for both office and residential use.

Istanbul today spreads across both the Asian and European shores of the Bosporus. A ceaseless flood of migrants from rural Anatolia has swollen the population, forming the largest city in Turkey.

The population figure in 2022 was around 15.8 million, but unofficial estimates put it as high as 18 million. European Istanbul contains the historic and business heart of the city. Asian Istanbul is more residential and better laid out. The two sides are linked by three large suspension bridges and a road-tunnel, and a multitude of ferries, boats, and a rail line which runs under the Bosporus. High-rise apartment complexes line both coasts as far as the eye can see. Around both parts of the city there is an unregulated jumble of housing built by migrants from the countryside alongside out-of-town satellite luxury developments of villas and apartments.

Istanbul is no longer the political capital of Turkey, but it is the cultural and economic center, and the commercial hub of the country. High-rise office

Istanbul's Eminönü district overlooking the Bosporus.

complexes, shopping malls, and modern art galleries
abut ancient monuments and museums and galleries
housing the treasures of former ages. The embassies
are in Ankara, but many consulates service Istanbul.
The AKP government has designated part of the Asian
side of Istanbul as a financial services center, including
a controversial decision to move the Central Bank
from Ankara to this new office development, called

the Istanbul International Financial Center (IIFC), as part of the government's goal to establish Istanbul as a global center for finance.

A growing city, Istanbul is rapidly trying to develop its infrastructure to keep pace with its burgeoning population. Construction is underway everywhere. One visitor was heard to exclaim, "Istanbul will be great once it is finished!"

Ankara Castle, first constructed in the seventh century BCE.

Ankara

The capital, Ankara, has experienced phenomenal growth in recent years. It is the seat of government and of all of the ministries, and is the second-largest city, with a population of over 5.7 million in 2022. It was home to Atatürk after he became leader of the movement for a free state, and has been the capital since 1923. Before then it was a sleepy Anatolian village, famous for the angora (Ankara) goat.

Ankara is situated on a plateau 3,000 feet (914 meters) above sea level. A city of bureaucrats, it is somewhat overshadowed by the expansive and cosmopolitan city of Istanbul, and remains in a way more provincial. It is well laid out with wide boulevards, parks, and public amenities. Foreign embassies are located here. There is a friendly rivalry between the business elite of Istanbul and their bureaucratic masters in Ankara: many Istanbulites maintain that the best thing about Ankara is the road back to Istanbul.

Izmir

Turkey's third-largest city, with a population of over 4 million, is Izmir, the pearl of the Aegean. It has been a major port since biblical times when it was known as Smyrna. Today it is home to an important NATO naval base, as well as to an annual trade fair. The sea-front promenade is lined with cafés and there is a real modern feel to the city. Many of the figs eaten in northern Europe at Christmas will have come from Izmir and it is also a major tobacco producer.

Izmir, the pearl of the Aegean.

GOVERNMENT

Based on its constitution, Turkey is a democratic, secular republic. In 2017 constitutional reforms introduced an executive presidency system under which a president is chosen directly by the electorate every five years. Prior to the reforms, the country operated according to a system of a parliamentary democracy whereby the president was appointed by parliamentary majority and crucially, had more limited powers. As part of the reforms, presidents are currently limited to serving a maximum of two terms.

The passing of constitutional reforms was not without some controversy, and in a public referendum on the matter was approved by only a slim majority of 52 percent. Under the previous parliamentary system the president was nonpartisan and did not set the political agenda or lead government—this was done by the prime minister and the Council of Ministers. The president's main role was largely limited to ensuring that the constitution was not violated, and that the government functioned properly. Under the changes, the office of prime minister was abolished, making the president now the head of government as well as head of state. The vice president and all cabinet members are now appointed by the president, as are high level executives of public institutions and university presidents. In addition, the new system allows the president to retain ties to a political party, seeing nonpartisanship of the role removed.

Turkey's parliament, the Grand National Assembly, is democratically elected. Its six hundred deputies serve five-year terms. Under the new laws, the leader of the party that wins the most seats is appointed speaker of the assembly. The role of parliament is to pass legislation, to set the budget, and to hold the cabinet accountable.

Some readers may be surprised to learn that Turkish law is not based on Islamic, or Sharia, law, but on the Swiss code, which means that an act is illegal until specifically enabled by a body of law.

Before an election the streets are covered in banners bearing the logos of political parties, and vans and buses drive around with loudspeakers blaring out lively music and promises for change. Often there are more than ten parties campaigning at one time. The parties range from conservative nationalists and fundamentalist Islamists on the right to the far left. Political parties in Turkey are prone to splitting and changing due to internal differences and power struggles. Sometimes they are shut down for illegal activities, and the same faces resurface later in a new party with a new name.

The judiciary is independent of the legislature but not of the government, with judges being appointed by the High Council of Judges and Prosecutors (HSYK), which falls under the control of the Justice Ministry. There are systems of criminal and administrative courts, including the Constitutional Court, the Supreme Court of Appeals, the Council of State, the Supreme Council of Public Accounts, the Supreme

Military Administrative Tribunal, the Military Court of Appeal, the Court of Jurisdictional Disputes, and the Supreme Electoral Board.

The Role of the Army

Until the constitutional referendum of 2017, the army played an important role as the guarantor of Atatürk's republic. A National Security Council met regularly, headed by the president, and attended by government ministers and senior officers in the armed services. Under the previous constitution, if the military believed that the government had acted in an unconstitutional way, it was allowed to step in. After the military coup in 1980, for example, the general public was relieved, because the military restored civil, fiscal, and legal order and enacted the 1982 Constitution defining the government's powers. The military's presence in national affairs was often viewed with suspicion by the West, but it was probably one of the main reasons Turkey has remained a democratic nation.

The Ergenekon trials (see page 36) severely weakened the Turkish army's role in political life, as did subsequent constitutional reform: the military is subject to investigation by the now civilian-majority National Security Council, the jurisdiction of military courts has been restricted to dealing with internal disciplinary matters, and martial law has been abolished.

Local Government

There are eighty-one provinces, divided into municipalities and villages. Every province has a governor, responsible for the departments of law enforcement, education, and citizenship. The police monitor cities and towns, the gendarmes (military police) the rural areas. The municipality supervises the fire department, local transportation, public amenities, and refuse collection.

THE ECONOMY

When Atatürk came to power the economy was mainly agricultural and most people lived in rural areas. Atatürk led a drive for modernization, and the early Republican era had an air of enterprise. New industries were founded. These included state-owned manufacturing and service companies such as tobacco- or sugar-processing plants, oil refineries, iron and steel factories, banks, and insurance companies. Turkey has made progress and today has a mixed economy with a strong tertiary sector (banking, finance, computers, consulting, etc.), a manufacturing base (in particular, textiles, and car manufacture), and agricultural and other raw material industries (such as cotton, marble, tobacco, citrus fruits, and wheat).

Turkey has become the breadbasket of the Middle East. It exports perishable items to Europe and the USA as well as to its neighbors. It is one of the world's main providers of hazelnuts, pistachios, and textiles. Turkish construction, transportation, and engineering companies are active in the Middle East and Central Asia.

During the 1980s and 1990s the economy was stagnant. Inflation soared and Turks suffered under the drastic corrective devaluation of the Turkish Lira (TL). Due to changes in fiscal policy, from 2002 the market stabilized, inflation fell, and Turkey was able to weather the global financial crisis of 2008.

Turkey's economy continued to improve, with credit rating agencies upgrading the country to "investment grade" in 2013. Cities in Anatolia are booming—under the AKP government Turkey has seen the rise of so-called "green capital companies," green being the color of conservative Islam. Many retail and industrial companies have sprung up with this type of ownership, and Islamic-style banking is now available in Turkey.

Toward the end of 2021 Turkey's currency slid and inflation soared once again. Unlike the crises of the 1980s and 1990s, however, this was a direct result of government policy intended to reduce interest rates in order to make Turkish-made goods more attractive abroad. This was a bold bid to encourage local and international investment in Turkish manufacturing to rival China and other Asian countries. The short-term results of this policy have caused a lot of pain for many, and it is still too early to tell whether it will improve Turkey's competitive position and lead to increased exports and employment in the long run.

COVID-19

When reports of a new respiratory illness emerged from China in early 2020, the Turkish government sprang into action in a bid to keep the virus at bay. Thermal cameras were installed at airports, flights from China were banned, and the land border with Iran, where large outbreaks had been recorded, was sealed. Inevitably, by March, Turkey had recorded its first local cases of Covid-19 and numbers rose sharply as the pandemic spread through the country as it did the world.

Throughout the pandemic, the government's stated aim was to do what it could to keep the economy going while protecting society's most vulnerable. This resulted in policies such as limiting the hours that those under the age of twenty and those over sixty-five could be outside their homes, periodic closures of cafés, restaurants, shopping malls, sports, and other leisure facilities, as well as limitations on travel to and from coronavirus hotspots around the world. Turkey moved swiftly to offer free vaccinations to the elderly and vulnerable as they became available, starting first with China's Sinopharm shot, and then later with Pfizer, referred to locally by the name of the company that developed the vaccine, BioNTech, which is run by German-Turk Uğur Şahin. At the end of 2021 Turkey's own vaccine, Turkovac, was approved for use, and by February 2022 more than 80 percent of the adult population had been double vaccinated.

An efficient app-based track and trace system supported the country's vaccination drive and allowed businesses to continue to operate, albeit at a reduced rate. Leisure, retail, and food and drink industries were hit in particular, and severely so during the periods of lockdown, but following the widespread administration of vaccines there has been some return to normality. Tourism, one of the mainstays of the economy, suffered greatly as a result of international travel restrictions, but signs in early 2022 showed that tourists were already beginning to return in increasing numbers, a very welcome sign for the Turkish economy.

INTERNATIONAL RELATIONS

Turkey has always been influenced by both East and West. Today, it is a member of the United Nations, the Organization for Economic Cooperation and Development, the North Atlantic Treaty Organization, and the Islamic Conference, and is still officially a candidate for European Union membership despite setbacks to its campaign in recent years.

Before the fall of Communism and the breakup of the Soviet Union, Turkey was of great strategic importance to the West as it formed the eastern boundary of NATO. A NATO fleet was based in Izmir, and the airbases of Adana and Batman, and Istanbul (guarding the Bosporus and access to the Black Sea), were vital strategic assets.

With the transition from the Cold War to the War on Terror, Turkey again became an important strategic international partner. As one of the few truly democratic Islamic nations, it is viewed by many as a model for outward-looking Islam, and an example of peaceful coexistence between the Christian and Muslim worlds—the West also recognizes the value of Turkey's strong cultural links with Central Asia and the Islamic world.

A number of Turkey's current relationships with key regional powers require skillful management in light of the country's own domestic needs and international interests. Turkey maintains business relations with China, despite the ongoing controversy regarding Turkic Uyghurs in China's Xinjiang province and a Uyghur diaspora resident in Turkey. Turkey and Russia collaborate in many sectors, despite deep ambivalence toward Turkey's trading partner among its NATO allies (Russia is Turkey's single most important energy provider, while many Turkish companies operate in Russia). Bilateral relations with Europe and the USA too have been strained in recent years, with key issues including the West's support of Kurdish forces in Syria, and America's refusal to extradite the exiled cleric Fethullah Gülen.

Turkey's large Muslim population means it is often feared by the West and wooed at the same time. Nowhere is this more evident than in the response to Turkey's application to join the European Union. Despite working to fulfill numerous joining requirements set by the EU, progress has largely stalled. In response President Erdoğan has pivoted Turkey's focus eastward and toward becoming a regional power instead.

A new airport has been built in Istanbul as part of Turkey's successful strategy to become a major transport hub, while energy pipelines flow through Turkish territory connecting east with west. In addition, Turkey now maintains its "summer clock" year-round; while this has helped to ease communication with eastern countries, it has increased the time difference with western countries.

Cyprus

The Mediterranean island of Cyprus has been fought over for centuries, but the present crisis has its roots in the 1960s. The island's population is a mix of Muslim Turks and Orthodox Greeks. In the latter half of the twentieth century, by the terms of the 1959 Treaty of London, Britain, Greece, and Turkey shared political responsibility for the stability and security of Cyprus. During the 1960s tension between the two communities increased, with killings and bloody reprisals. The Turkish minority felt underrepresented and feared that the Greek majority wanted Cyprus to join Greece.

Increased intercommunal violence and a coup by extreme right-wing Greek officers of the Cypriot National Guard against the government of President Makarios led Turkish Prime Minister Bülent Ecevıt to send troops into Cyprus in 1974. Turkey considered itself to be acting in accordance with the Treaty of London, in defense of Turkish Cypriot lives and liberty. The Western world saw this act as an invasion. Stalemate on the ground led to the division of the island into two parts separated by a demilitarized zone. The northern, Turkish part declared itself the Turkish Federated State of Cyprus, and was recognized by Turkey.

The rest of the world regarded the new state as illegitimate, and only recognized the government of the southern, Greek part.

Despite various attempts to reach a political settlement on the island, the old enmity between Greeks and Turks continues. In 2004 a referendum was held on the question of reuniting the island. In a reversal of their previously entrenched positions, the Turkish population voted "yes" to unification and the Greek population voted "no." The inclusion of Cyprus in the EU has caused more political difficulties than it has solved, and the issue of a divided Cyprus looks set to remain for some time.

CHAPTER TWO

VALUES *&* ATTITUDES

Turkish society is extremely polarized today between those whose attitudes and values are secular, and those whose are Islamic. Conservative Muslims find some aspects of modern secularism difficult to accept, while Kemalist secularists find some elements of the Islamic tradition equally problematic.

The clash of culture and debates between these two viewpoints dominate the social and political scene, as they have done for some years now. In early 2013 the argument over what is Turkey's national drink raged for days after the prime minister said it should be the yogurt-based "*ayran*" rather than the alcoholic drink "*rakı*."

While it is difficult to provide general descriptions that will be accurate for both halves of Turkish society, beyond the religious divide there are deep underlying values shared by all Turks, the most important of which are described in this chapter.

RESPECT AND HONOR

Turkish culture places great emphasis on respect, honor, and pride. This is a society where "old-fashioned" manners are still practiced to some degree, though university students and young adults tend to be less formal. Last names are rarely used; instead, titles are applied to the first name as signs of respect or relationship. It is rude to call a new acquaintance by his or her first name only. It is polite, depending on the situation, to use either *amca* or *teyze* (uncle or aunt), or *bey* or *hanım* (sir or madam), after the person's first name. A young adult will be addressed by children and youth as *abla* (elder sister) or *ağabey* (big brother), alone or after their given name. If you are an instructor, educator, or teacher, you may be called by your first name followed by *hoca* (teacher), pronounced "hodja."

Seniority is owed considerable respect in Turkey; young people will pay visits to their elders on special holidays first, and will be actively concerned with their well-being. Gray-haired visitors may find themselves treated especially well.

Honor is important and Turkish culture is strongly hierarchical and patriarchal. Individuals are ranked according to status. Age is significant in determining this. Determining relative status by age, however, also depends on the older person's perception of himself. A visitor in his twenties who, with honorable intentions, addresses a man in his forties as "uncle," when that man may prefer to be called "brother," may elicit some teasing from his friends, but the general rule is that until the foreigner knows how a person wishes to be treated, it is best to err on the side of caution and show more honor rather than less.

Showing Respect

Showing respect is vital in Turkey. People who are honored may have gained power because of their individual reputation, family, wealth, and political or religious leadership. In the simplest of terms, people in positions of authority will be honored by those under them; for example, an employer will be treated deferentially by an employee, and a teacher will be honored by a student.

It is important to know how and when to honor others. For example, when entering a room, be sure to greet all who are present. Not affirming status in the appropriate situations can have detrimental consequences for relationships and one's own reputation. For example, you shouldn't turn your back on a person of importance as it can be considered deeply insulting. Neither should you disagree with or correct them in public.

Many Turks smoke a lot. However, they will not do so in front of an older person, as a sign of respect, and so don't be surprised if someone leaves the room for a few minutes to smoke a cigarette. Arguing or challenging an older person in public is also considered bad form.

Another area of honor is related to the family. The family's good name depends much on the honor and modesty of the women and their virtuous behavior and/or the family's economic status. Loss of face can be detrimental to relatives. If honor is questioned and the family's reputation is damaged, family members are responsible for restoring the family's honor by ostracizing the member in question.

Harmony is a supreme value in Turkey, and as a result, where they may challenge a harmonious relationship, frankness and honesty are not seen as positive attributes. Many Turks feel that it is impolite to speak as directly as some foreigners do—if you are unsure whether your comments may cause offence (directly or indirectly), it may be better to keep quiet. If directness causes someone to lose face and makes him feel that his feelings are not valued, he may not forget or forgive. It is also possible that those who witness the incident may not forget or forgive either. A person who feels insulted may hold a grudge for a lifetime.

Turks generally appear very confident. In order to save face, it is common not to admit to a weakness or mistake. Shifting blame is expected. Self-disclosure happens only with close friends.

Dignity

Dignity, not to be confused with honor, but as important, should always be preserved. For example, a request for a substantial favor will be made indirectly or by a third party. Visitors who are used to more directness must learn not to give straight refusals or a frank "no." Such a direct reply would cause the person who has made the request to lose face. If possible, it is best to give an answer that causes no embarrassment to either party. If rejecting the request, it is advisable to put the blame on an outside cause and avoid possible personal offense.

You may think of this, or of the use of a third party in making a request, as being manipulative. Or, valuing frankness and directness, you may interpret polite and indirect answers as being dishonest. It's important to understand that this is not so for your Turkish friend; rather, it is being kind and respectful of your honor and feelings, both of which take precedence.

FAMILY, FRIENDS, COMMUNITY

Turkish society is very group oriented. Group allegiance is paramount, and Turks will be faithful to the group on which they depend for their identity and support, as affirmed by the idiom "*Sevginin en güçlü hali ailedir*" ("The strongest form of love is family"), the meaning of which is that in the end, you know who your family are. It is a multifaceted value found in every sector of society. As polarization has deepened in recent years, one's group allegiance has become even more significant.

The social unit with the strongest demands on a person's loyalty is the family—the fundamental structure of life. The importance placed on family in Turkey is well expressed in the local proverb: "A sheep separated from the flock is eaten by wolves." The benefits and security afforded by one's family do not come without obligations, however. For example, the family expects deep loyalty in all aspects of life, social and otherwise. The eldest son always has a special place of responsibility, helping his father and caring for younger siblings in his father's absence. Children are treated with special indulgence when they are young. When they are grown they are truly a kind of social security for their parents. The family will naturally help each other in difficult circumstances, whether or not these are of the member's own making—for example, an older sister who works may support a younger brother who is unemployed.

Friendships are also important, and in Turkey these can involve great commitment and mutual concern, and a lot of time. To establish a true friendship takes effort; it is important to visit regularly and to help in times of need. Friends never betray one another, and friendships often include an expectation of mutual help. If a favor is done for someone, that person (and usually their family) will remember it.

Turkish people generally form friendships with others of the same sex, who are of a similar age and status. Usually, unequal economic or social status precludes deep friendship. If a man and woman are friends, they will refer to each other in kinship terms; for example, a woman would consider her husband's friend to be like her *kardeş* (brother) and not her *dost* (friend), which would imply an improperly familiar or possibly romantic relationship.

Though signs of individualism are growing, community is still highly valued. Neighbors and relatives help each other in many practical ways, such as by providing food or beds for each other's guests. If a crisis occurs, the support of one's community and neighbors is usually strong, and action arising from group affiliation rather than individualism is still the norm.

NATIONAL PRIDE

The phrase, "*Ne mutlu Türküm diyene!*" ("How happy is he or she who can say, I am Turkish!") is a common slogan in Turkey, and genuinely reflects most people's belief in and commitment to their nation and

People celebrating Çocuk Bayramı, National Sovereignty and Children's Day.

homeland. A recent survey by one Turkish university saw more than 85 percent of citizens in Central Anatolia describe themselves as "proud Turks" (though this figure fell to 23 percent in the largely Kurdish populated regions of the south-east).

Mustafa Kemal Atatürk restored to the Turks pride in their nationality and homeland. This is deep-seated and expresses itself in some surprising ways—for example, it is an offense to wear a garment made out of the flag. A beloved TV presenter once outraged the national press by kicking a balloon that had the crescent and star on it during a program celebrating Republic Day. It is a serious insult to make jokes about the national anthem, the flag, or Atatürk. Turks may be critical of their own nation or government, but they will not like it if you agree with them or make negative statements yourself.

More extreme expressions of national pride can be seen in right-wing parties such as the MHP (Nationalist Action Party), which, with its slogan of "Turkey for the Turks," is typically anti-Western and anti-foreigner. The party uses as its symbol a wolf and the crescent and star, and supporters at political rallies may make a hand sign portraying a wolf.

ATATÜRK, SECULARISM, AND RELIGION

Although Atatürk, in a complete break with the past, established a secular government, Islam continues to have a pivotal role in the life and character of the nation.

Turkish society can be broadly divided into four subgroups: Atatürk supporters (secularists), Leftists, Islamic fundamentalists, and modern Islamists. Understanding these different segments of society is important for whomever you meet and interact with.

Atatürk supporters uphold links with the West and look for modernization at every opportunity. They are educated, middle-class, progressive citizens who are Muslim. They oppose Islamic law, believing it to be backward and dangerous.

They revere Atatürk, and often can be heard to mourn that there is no one like him today. They are fiercely loyal to the values of democracy, liberalization, and modernization that he championed.

Atatürk supporters wear lapel pins bearing his image, visit the Anıtkabir (his mausoleum in Ankara), and quote his speeches. His picture hangs in most public buildings and many important public places such as dams and roadways are named after him. Evidence of Kemal Atatürk is everywhere, and first-time visitors to Turkey may mistakenly equate this with the leadership cult of former communist countries. However, veneration of Atatürk, while encouraged by the school system, is not imposed.

The second subgroup is known as Muslim Socialists. These are Turks who hold left-wing political views, who are anti-Western, and most often are not devout Muslims. It is worth noting too that the Kurdish terrorist group, PKK, is also ideologically Marxist.

The third subgroup is the Islamic fundamentalists. They often strongly disagree with the followers of

Atatürk and wish to see the nation return to Islamic values, believing that the five pillars of Islam and Islamic law should be diligently practiced. They are uncomfortable with the notion of a secular state and would support, to varying degrees, integration of state and religion. They promote religious-based activities like wearing headscarves and teaching Arabic and the Koran to children, both of which are opposed to by secularists.

The fourth subgroup is modern Islamists. This subgroup emerged in the last thirty years and consists of well-educated, middle-class individuals who defer to Islamic rather than secular values. For example, modern Islamists oppose alcohol, clubs, and provocative dress such as miniskirts and low-cut dresses, and support the wearing of headscarves. In social settings they tend to separate men and women. Their use of language is influenced by Islamic terminology and Ottoman Turkish, Arabic, and Persian loan words.

Modern Islamists support the AK Party, which, while attempting to lessen the separation of state and religion, still seeks closer links with the wider world. An important grassroots organization among modern Islamists was the "Hizmet" group, an organization with links to the Turkish Muslim teacher Fethullah Gülen who currently lives in exile in America. The group was very influential and ran many schools, businesses, and media conglomerates in Turkey. However, after the failed attempted coup of 2016, tens of thousands of Gülenists, including high-ranking soldiers and judges, were arrested and their assets confiscated.

THE FIVE PILLARS OF ISLAM

- The creed, called *shahada* (meaning testimony or witness): a person who recites "There is no god but Allah and Muhammad is his prophet" three times will be considered a Muslim.
- Prayer five times a day.
- Observation of the annual fast during the month of Ramadan.
- Giving of alms.
- The Hajj: every Muslim should make the pilgrimage to Mecca at least once during his or her lifetime.

ISLAM

"To be a Turk is to be a Muslim" is a statement that defines both nationality and culture; in Turkey today, more than 99 percent of the population are Muslim, even though they may not be practicing Muslims.

Islam is both a faith and a way of life, an integral belief system that is both religious and political. God, or Allah, is recognized as the creator of everything in the universe and is the ultimate source of *ruh* (life spirit).

The Koran is the holy book of Islam and is understood to be the written word of God as revealed to the Prophet Muhammad, who recited the chapters (or *suras*) of the Koran to scribes for notation. The Koran is sacred and is considered one of the most

Interior of the Holy Hagia Sophia Grand Mosque, Istanbul.

beautiful works in Arabic literature. Many Muslim traditions and practices are contained not in the Koran, but in the Hadith: a written record of what the Prophet Muhammad said, did, or approved.

Perhaps the most noticeable element of Islam for visitors is the call to prayer (*ezan*) that echoes across Turkey's towns and villages. The five daily prayers are held at sunrise, noon, mid-afternoon, sunset, and after nightfall. The call is in Arabic and starts with the statement "*Allah-u Akbar*," which means, "God is great." The call to prayer is given by a muezzin, who is specially trained in the melody of the chant. The muezzin used to have to climb stairs to the top of the minaret, but as technology has developed, the muezzin may now sit below and use a microphone and loudspeakers. Often the prayer calls of different mosques start just seconds after each other, creating something of a chorus around the city, reminding the faithful of their obligations.

The mosque is the primary community space for Islamic teaching and religious activity. The imam is both prayer leader and teacher at the mosque. The majority of Turkish Muslims are from the mainstream Sunni tradition. Among the well-known smaller groups or sects present in Turkey are the Sufis and Alevis. Both groups appreciate and use music as part of their worship, and their beliefs include mysticism.

The Alevis, who are Shiites, comprise about 10–15 percent of the population. They differ from Sunnis in that they believe the line of the Caliphate goes through Ali, the cousin and son-in-law of the Prophet Muhammad. Instead of the mosque, they worship and meet in the *cemevi,* or community hall. Men and women are permitted to sit in the same *cemevi*, although they are segregated. Meals, music, and dance are part of their communal worship. Their leaders are known as *pir* (spiritual leader) and *dede* (a senior Dervish).

NEW RELIGIOUS STRUCTURES

Turkish Islam used to be centrally led by the Sultan in his capacity as Caliph, spiritual leader of all Muslims. The caliphate was abolished by Atatürk, but the state still oversees religious matters through the Department of Religious Affairs, which is today under the authority of the president. Article 136 of the Turkish constitution established this department to oversee the principles of belief, worship, and moral standards in Turkey "in accordance with the principles of secularism, removed from all political views and ideas and aiming at national solidarity and integrity." During the 2000s the department's staff doubled and the budget significantly increased. It appoints and trains all religious leaders. A Muslim scholar, or mufti, is appointed head in each province and county; this individual oversees all the imams and rules on points of observance, in accordance with the principles laid down by the Department of Religious Affairs.

All religious education is given either through Koran schools licensed by the Department of Religious Affairs, or through the state education system (schools and universities) run by the Department of National Education. In recent years there has been an increase in the number of single-sex religious-based middle and high schools opened by the Department of Education.

Questions of Islamic practice are settled with reference to the Department of Religious Affairs, and their Web site provides details on the daily times for the call to prayer, a verse and Hadith saying for the day, and the opportunity to e-mail your religious questions to an expert.

EDUCATION

Urban middle- and upper-class Turks place great importance on education, and parents will encourage their children to work hard in order to secure a well-paid job in the future.

Children must attend school for twelve years (up from eight years prior to 2012) beginning at the age of six. This new model sees students required to complete four years at elementary, middle, and high school each. In Turkey, public and private schools are available, though in many areas public schools have exceptionally large classes. Kindergarten (*yuva*) and preschool (*anaokul*) are always private.

Education is controlled by the National Ministry of Education (Milli Eğitim Bakanlığı). The elementary school week begins and ends with the national anthem. A controversial change, not supported by secularists, was the removal of the daily promise to uphold Atatürk's principles, reciting: "I am a Turk, I am right, I am hard-working. My guiding principles are to protect those weaker than me, to respect my elders and to love my land and my nation more than I love myself. My country is on the ascent and advancing. O, great Atatürk, I swear that I will constantly walk in the way which you created for me and toward the goal which you showed me. May my whole being be a gift to the Turkish nation. How blessed is he who can say, 'I am a Turk.'"

The number of private schools and universities has increased significantly in recent years, causing the education system to undergo many changes. In line with society's increasing polarization, most private schools have a philosophical slant that is either more secular or Islamic. For decades students learned by rote. However, more recently, there has been a gradual move toward more experimental approaches. Turkish schools tend to be strong on math, Turkish language, history, religion, and citizenship. Competition to pass entrance exams for high schools and university is fierce. Turkish children have a lot of homework and take extra classes on the weekend. Parents often put great pressure on them to gain better marks for acceptance in schools where lessons are taught in German, English, or French.

Today, more women are graduating from Turkish universities and entering the professional sector than ever before. In 2021 about half of all university students were women, and Turkish universities had a higher proportion of women lecturers than in either the European Union or the USA. Many universities teach

Students at Istanbul University celebrate their graduation.

in foreign languages and offer two- and four-year
degree programs.

WOMEN IN SOCIETY

The role of women in society has changed drastically
over the centuries. As the level of education increases,
the idea that women are important only for serving
men's needs and for childbearing is diminishing.
Topkapı Palace with its sultan's harem is now just a
tourist site. As you walk down the street you can see a
mix of women, from those in headscarves to miniskirted
office employees relaxing in a sushi bar after work.
Women drive privately owned cars—but we have yet to
see a woman driving a truck or bus! They run companies.
They are top models, TV presenters, and politicians. In
the 1990s, Turkey had a female prime minister.

   The civil code enacted in 1926 abolished polygamy
and introduced a minimum age for marriage. It also
gave equality of inheritance and made a woman's
testimony as valid as a man's in a court of law. Atatürk
gave women the right to vote in 1930—earlier than in
many European countries.

   Promotion is often readily available on merit for
women working in industry and offices. The glass
ceiling so often complained of elsewhere in Europe
is less in evidence in the modern Turkish company.
Educated middle- and upper-class women fill many
important roles in professional fields such as finance,
law, and medicine.

Some Turkish women define their roles in domestic terms as a good mother and wife. In towns, villages, or lower-class areas, many women would describe their main role as that of tension manager in the home. The mother is the person to whom all have access, acting as mediator between father and children and generally attempting to ease the strains created by social change.

The importance of a woman maintaining her honor is crucial. It is believed that proper behavior between men and women depends most of all on the woman. Chastity is taken very seriously, though in some respects, the standard for men is not the same as for women. Improper behavior can result in family ostracism or even more serious action, the most extreme being a decision by the family elders to appoint a male relative as summary executioner, though this is increasingly rare.

Although things are gradually changing, particularly for educated women, some traditional rules may still apply: for example, in more religiously conservative circles, it is unusual for a woman to live on her own: a female relative will likely join her, or she will be invited to a relative's home.

In general, when in public, women should take care to be reserved and restrained in their demeanor, and avoid over-friendly smiles, eye contact, and casual friendliness in social settings of mixed company. Not doing so runs the risk of diminishing one's honor and attracting unwanted advances as a result. In a work context this may vary, depending on the situation and status of the people involved.

MEMLEKET AND *HEMŞEHRİ*

The concepts of hometown, *memleket*, and fellow countrymen, *hemşehri*, are important in Turkey. Even with tremendous migration to towns and cities, Turks rarely lose their ties with the past, so much so that even those born in urban centers may identify themselves as being from a different part of the country, where their family roots are. The words of a Turkish song capture this loyalty and identity perfectly: "There is a village far away; whether we go there or not it is still our village."

In addition, people will also have a sense of loyalty toward those who are from the same area. In most big cities, there are social clubs where people from a particular region can meet and provide each other mutual help and support.

CHAPTER THREE

CUSTOMS & TRADITIONS

NATIONAL HOLIDAYS

Turkey has many national holidays, and if one falls
on a weekend a working day is not given in lieu. The
Turkish official calendar is the Western Gregorian
one and the non-religious national holidays are
on fixed dates, many of which commemorate a
significant event in the Atatürk era. The religious
holidays are based on the Muslim lunar calendar
and so their dates change each year. During most
holidays many people travel, either to see their
family in other parts of the country or to take
a vacation in Turkey or abroad. During such
periods, intercity buses and air flights can become
fully booked weeks in advance. The roads are
often crowded and unfortunately the incidence of
accidents often increases.

New Year's Day: January 1

While fundamentalist Muslims discourage the celebration of this holiday, secular Muslim Turks enjoy a family gathering similar to how Christmas is celebrated in Europe and America. After all, Father Christmas is based on Saint Nicholas, who came from the Myra/Antalya region of Turkey! Christmas trees and decorations are put up, and families exchange presents and have a turkey dinner on New Year's Eve. If you are working in Turkey, an appropriate business gift at this time is a New Year's basket, with food items such as chocolate, coffee, cheese, fruit, and even alcohol or a pack of cigarettes (depending on where the recipient stands on the secular/Islamic polemic!). In general, flowers and chocolates are a good gift at any time of year. Gifts for friends can be purchased for delivery on online stores like Çiçek Sepeti (www.ciceksepeti.com).

Çocuk Bayramı: April 23

National Sovereignty and Children's Day commemorates the day that Atatürk convened the Grand National Assembly during the War of Independence. Schools have special ceremonies and parades, and poems about Atatürk are recited. In addition, children from around the world are flown to Ankara to participate in an annual international and national folklore ceremony.

Many hang flags to mark the occasion, while office buildings may have huge flags, or a picture of Atatürk draped over them. Officials visit the Anıtkabir mausoleum in Ankara, where Atatürk is buried. Similar ceremonies are held at the Atatürk statue in each city, though the size of the ceremony and related street decorations will depend on where the local municipality stands on the secularist-religious divide.

Labor Day: May 1
This international holiday is observed on May 1st to commemorate the achievements of the labor movement.

Gençlik Bayramı: May 19
Youth and Sport Day commemorates Atatürk's landing in Samsun to organize the revolution and start the War of Independence. Sports arenas host a parade of young people, with folk dancing, sporting displays, and speeches, while ceremonies take place in town squares. In the past few years this holiday has not been as widely celebrated as it once was, with the exception of the city of Samsun, where a whole neighborhood and also the university are called "19th May."

Demokrasi Günü: July 15
Democracy and Celebration of Freedom Day is a new holiday instituted in remembrance of those injured or killed resisting the failed coup attempt of 2016.

Zafer Bayramı: August 30
This commemorates the victory in the War of Independence when foreign powers were expelled from Turkish soil. A military parade is held in Ankara, and in Istanbul navy and helicopter fleets display along the

Bosporus. Ceremonies are held at the statue of Atatürk
in every city and dignitaries visit the Anıtkabir. Civic
parades are held in the evening, often by torchlight,
along main streets.

Cumhüriyet Bayramı: October 29

This is the anniversary of the day the Republic was
founded. Flags are hung and ceremonies are held to
commemorate Atatürk and the Republic. As with
Çocuk Bayramı and Gençlik Bayramı, it is more
enthusiastically celebrated by pro-Atatürk secularists.

Children taking part in a Republic Day ceremony.

November 10

This is not a holiday, but there is a minute of silence
at 9:05 a.m. to mark the anniversary of the passing of
Atatürk. If you are in public, stop what you are doing,

and stand to attention in silence. Fire alarms and sirens will go off, and drivers will hoot their horns.

RELIGIOUS HOLIDAYS

These change each year in line with the lunar Muslim calendar, which is about eleven days shorter than the Gregorian one, meaning that the holidays move forward each year. The civil authorities determine how many days the civil holiday should last and if the timing means that there is just one working day between the weekend and the holiday, it may be decided to join the two together and make one long week of holiday.

Feast of Sacrifice (Kurban Bayramı: Eid al-Adha)

This is the most important religious holiday of the year. It lasts for four days and commemorates the Koranic story in which the patriarch Abraham shows the ultimate act of submission to the will of Allah (Islam means "submission") by being prepared to sacrifice his son. God stops him and instead leads him to sacrifice a ram. (This is similar to the biblical account, except that in Islam the son is Ishmael, not Isaac.)

The story is commemorated by the sacrifice of an animal on the first day of the holiday, immediately after morning prayer. Recent changes in public health laws mean it is illegal for people to sacrifice an animal in their backyard—the municipality provides locations for livestock purchase and for professionals to carry out the sacrifices. The meat is given to the poor and needy, and shared with neighbors and friends.

Ramadan

Known locally as Ramazan, this holy month of fasting is referred to as "sultan of the other eleven months." It is a mandatory fast; individuals can also voluntarily fast at other times of the year. Practicing Muslims abstain from food, drink, sex, and smoking during the hours of daylight. These depend on the time of year: in the winter the days are shorter, so the fast is easier than when it occurs in summer. Calendars are printed showing the exact times at which the fast begins in the morning and ends in the evening. These times vary from city to city across Turkey: Istanbul and Izmir in the west will begin the fast later than Trabzon and Diyarbakır in the east. Children, travelers, pregnant women, and the sick are exempt. A lot of preparation is necessary: women clean their houses from top to bottom and fully stock their larders for the traditional meals.

People who are fasting can get up early before sunrise for a meal called *sahur*. Drummers go up and down the street beating drums as a warning that the sun is about to rise, and that it is the last chance to eat before daylight. At the end of the month, the drummers try to ring every doorbell, expecting to get a tip.

Each day the fast is broken at sundown with a meal called *iftar*, which begins with a prayer. A date or olive is usually eaten to break the fast—Muhammad

İftar: families and friends break the daily fast during the month of Ramazan.

traditionally used dates—and there are several ways of knowing when the moment to eat has arrived: lights on the minarets of mosques are lit up, and in the past, mosques would fire a live cannon (the "Ramazan *topu*"), though today fireworks have become more common. The television is also widely used: a ticker tape at the bottom of the screen shows the exact time of *iftar* for each town. During the hour leading up to and after the breaking of the fast, television programs usually focus on religious subjects—pictures of mosques, Islamic music, debates between Muslim scholars, and Koran chanting.

Keeping the fast in hot weather is difficult, but perhaps it is hardest for cigarette smokers. Just before *iftar*, tempers can flare, and traffic jams increase as everyone rushes to where they'll be breaking the fast. (Don't try to get a taxi as they will not be interested in picking up passengers!) Extensive physical labor is not generally expected during this month.

İftar meals can often be large and lavish, and despite it being a month of fasting, sometimes people end up eating more during Ramadan than in normal months. You may expect there to be little interest in food during a month of fasting, but the reverse is true; women take great pride in preparing their best cuisine for the *iftar* meals. Magazines are full of recipe ideas, and afternoon TV shows have celebrity chefs hosting cooking programs. It is an honor to be invited to an iftar meal, and one should never refuse.

Ramadan is also an important time for almsgiving. Local authorities will erect a Ramadan tent in the center of town providing a free *iftar* meal for the needy. This can also be supported by contributions from wealthy donors.

There are Ramadan traditions: in the days of the sultans, it was a festival time. Dishes usually not seen at the rest of the year are served—Ramazan *pide*, a special bread, is delicious, and lines of fasters can form outside bakeries before *iftar*. In the evening during Ramadan more men are likely to go to the mosque, and local authorities put on traditional entertainment such as jugglers, firecrackers, and puppet shows. Businesses and organizations may also host an *iftar* meal at a hotel or restaurant for important contacts.

Not all Turks participate in the Ramadan fast, and so restaurants and cafés in big cities often remain open. It is considerate not to eat in the street, however. You may be offered water or tea in business meetings or in a shop during Ramadan and it is not offensive to accept, even if some present are fasting; it is seen as being of extra value to fast when someone else is drinking. If you ask someone whether they are fasting or not, those fasting will say "*niyetliyim*," which means "I intend" (to complete the fast). The correct reply to this is "*Allah kabul etsin*"—"May God accept it."

Ramadan Holiday (Şeker Bayramı: Eid al-Fitr)

This is a three-day feast to celebrate the end of the month of Ramadan. The Turkish name means "sugar holiday." Everyone buys candy to give as presents or to hand out to children who knock on their door. The first day is reserved for family celebrations. The whole family gathers at the home of the oldest person to show respect and kiss the elder's hand. The children receive *bayram harç* (pocket money) from the older relatives. It is usual for the whole family to visit the graves of departed older relatives, and to pray for their souls.

In offices, chocolates are given to employees and business contacts.

Kandil

Kandil days are commemorative days that are not holidays from work. These days of particular religious significance are Muhammad's birthday, the night of Muhammad's conception (believed to be a time to receive forgiveness and mercy), the Night of Forgiveness, the Night of Power and Destiny (the night the Koran was given to Muhammad), and the night of the Night Journey (when Muhammad visited heaven). Minarets are lit up for these occasions and a special ring pastry called *kandil simidi* is made. Religious programming on the television is also common at this time.

Devout Muslims may hold a religious ceremony (*mevlut*) at home. An *imam* (prayer leader), or, among certain sects, the *dede* (spiritual leader), both of whom can be called *hoca* (teacher), will lead chanting of the Koran and recite religious poems. Women wear headscarves and dress modestly. If you are present, remember that at one point the worshipers will turn to face Mecca.

There is a closing prayer and the guests' hands are sprinkled with rosewater. After the ceremony the host offers refreshments.

Other Religious Festivals

Other religious festivals are celebrated on a local basis around Turkey. For example, an Alevi holiday is held in the town of Hacıbektaş every August. This is a three-day celebration, attended by many Alevi Muslims, who camp in the area. It celebrates the teaching of Hacıbektaş, the founder of an important Dervish order in the twelfth century. The most famous saying of his is "Be master of your hand, your loins, and your tongue."

The Mevlana festival is held every December in Konya, where Dervishes dance in accordance with the teachings of the great mystic poet of Islam, Mevlana, also known as Rumi (1207–73). They wear white robes and conical hats, and twirl to drums and a shepherd's pipe. The mesmerizing circular dance represents the harmony of the spheres and is an expression of cosmic love.

The dancers hold one hand up to God and one hand down to the earth, symbolizing union with God through trance. This Sufi dance was banned under Atatürk. Recently, it has been revived as part of Turkey's social history.

Another significant annual religious event is the Hajj to Mecca. In smaller towns, it is common to have a big celebration to send people off and welcome them back. During the time of Hajj, the bus terminals and airports are packed with pilgrims, who can often be quite elderly, wearing the simple white robe. Those returning are called *hacı*—one who has done the Hajj. When someone has made the Hajj, it is good to visit the *hacı*, and in return you will receive a present such as prayer beads or water from the holy well in Mecca.

Aşure Time

This is a special time in the year when women prepare *aşure* pudding and give it to their neighbors. *Aşure* is known as Noah's pudding, and it is a sweet dessert cooked using all the grains and fruits that Noah was assumed to have taken into the ark.

Zeybek dancers performing at the Selçuk camel wrestling festival.

REGIONAL FESTIVALS

Regions have annual festivals, often linked with sport or with local agricultural produce, such as:
January: Selçuk (camel wrestling)
May: Silifke (music and folklore), Tekirdağ (cherry festival)
June: Bursa (silk festival)
July: Edirne (traditional grease wrestling), Akşehir Nasreddin Hoca festival
October: Antalya (international arts festival)
December: Demre festival (Saint Nicholas), Konya Mevlana festival.

Fighters grappling at the Edirne traditional grease wrestling tournament.

TURKISH TRADITIONS

As we have seen, to be a Turk today is to be a Muslim, and secular Turks will still call themselves Muslim, even though they do not attend the mosque regularly and may not uphold the five pillars of Islam as stringently or at all. They still participate in many of the customs, such as circumcision, and will join in some of the fast and special meals during Ramadan. This is done partly out of social solidarity; religious festivals and beliefs give a structure and a unity to social life, which is deeply valued by Turks.

Turkey is a country of diversity. There are the modernists and secularists who want to travel, shop, learn about other cultures, and try new ideas. Then there are others who are very traditional and pious. The women wear headscarves and the men have beards and carry prayer beads. There are thirty-three beads on a strand; by thumbing through it three times, one has recited the ninety-nine names of Allah. In practice, many men just fiddle with their beads, using them more as "worry beads." This is an example of a custom that is not directly in line with orthodox Muslim teaching but is derived from cultural practice. There are many similar examples in Turkish culture, some of which are fusions of Islam with the shamanism or folk religion of the Turks' nomadic ancestors.

Folklore and Superstition

Depending on economic and religious status, individuals can be quite superstitious. The "evil eye" is considered to be the main cause of many misfortunes, and blue and white beads and ornaments are used to protect against it. Blue eyes are also believed to be a natural protection against the evil eye.

A *cin*, pronounced "jinn," is believed by Muslims to be a living spirit or genie. These are always present around humans, but unseen. There are both good and evil jinns, who can cause sickness, insanity, or death. The majority of Turks fear them and take them seriously. For example, a common belief is that it is wrong to compliment a baby. Instead, Turks will purposely say that a baby is ugly, or call it *satılmış* ("sold") so the jinn will not want to steal it away or send it an illness. Similarly, it is believed that excessive praise may draw an evil jinn's attention to someone good, and cause the jinn to hurt the person out of jealousy. The word "*maşallah*" is used to ward off the evil eye and is often said after giving praise.

People often pray at saints' tombs for a good outcome. Different tombs are believed to be effective for different requests, such as good crops, conceiving, receiving healing, or finding a marriage partner. Normally when a Turk visits the tomb he makes a vow and a bargain with God and if his prayer comes true, he will perform a righteous deed. You'll notice that at a holy place, such as a shrine or tomb, Turks tie a string or a strip of cloth on a sacred tree to make a wish.

When out and about, you may see advertised in café windows: "We read coffee grounds." Turks are interested in all aspects of fortune-telling, by astrologers or gypsies, studying coffee grounds, or using rabbits. On the street you may see a man with a rabbit. You pay him for the rabbit to choose you a slip of paper, which tells your fortune.

Turks make a "tsk tsk" noise and/or pull an earlobe while knocking on a table for luck—a superstition similar to "knock on wood," which usually follows a wish about the future. Words such as "*inşallah*" ("God willing") are used to avoid tempting fate.

Curses are feared by many Turks and, since Turks can hold a grudge for life, they may well arrange for a curse to be put on a person they are upset with. A *hoca* is a Muslim shaman skilled in these things—luckily, he can also break a curse that someone is believed to have put on you!

The Koran is often placed on a high shelf in the home and is thought of as an amulet against evil. For example, women may sew paper inscribed with verses of the Koran into the folds of a sick person's clothes for healing. A Turk will recite the Bismillah, the first verse of the Koran, at the beginning of a journey, when scared, or at night before going to bed to ward off evil: "In the name of Allah, the most merciful, the most compassionate." The Bismillah is also often hung in homes, shops, offices, and restaurants.

For a blessing, an animal will sometimes be sacrificed at the start of something new, such as the foundation of a new building or opening of a new workplace.

Dreams are thought to be very significant in foretelling the future and some people are considered gifted in interpretation. It is not unusual for a friend to say, "I saw you in my dream last night," and attach some importance to this.

The concept of *kismet* has a major role in people's lives in Turkey. This is a belief in fate and in the predetermination of events, described by Turks as the "command of God"—a belief that one's personal needs, friendships, marriage, disasters, and accidents are all predestined. This mindset can sometimes lead Turks to appear passive in taking control of one's life and future planning. It also leads them to be accepting of their lot.

Two contrasting proverbs shed light on the degree of fatalism in different sections of Turkish society. One reads "I found food today, I'll eat today: Tomorrow? Ah well, God is great." This reflects a belief that all our accomplishments are only possible through the grace of Allah. The second teaches "First tie your camel to the tree, then pray to God for its protection"—that is, while ultimately the blessing comes from Allah, he expects you to play your part in making it happen.

The popular *nazar* amulet, believed to provide protection from the evil eye.

CHAPTER FOUR

MAKING FRIENDS

Visitors to Turkey will quickly find that people are very sociable, extremely hospitable, and that they will treat you with great warmth, particularly if you are visiting alone. In Turkey, "the more the merrier" is an abiding value and in general, people prefer to do things in groups rather than individually. So much so in fact that it's not always well understood why a person would want to spend time alone or be independent. Quite inevitably, the people you come to know will make an effort to look after you and make sure that you are not lonely.

One thing visitors should be aware of when it comes to making friends in Turkey, however, is that the immediate warmth and generosity you receive should not be mistaken for real friendship, which takes time to develop. Meaningful friendships in Turkey imply commitment, loyalty, and genuine concern. Friends are expected to see each other often and to be inquiring as to their well-being and that of their family. The concept of privacy in Turkey differs greatly from much of the West; someone who has been ill would expect you to want all the details of their doctor's visit, and if you don't ask will assume that it's because you don't care. Flowery language is common and appreciated, so expect to hear phrases like "I've missed you a lot," and you should use them too.

Phrase Your Questions with Care!

Turks don't like to disappoint people and as such, you should be careful how you phrase your questions to people. For example, an experienced shopper in an Istanbul market would not ask, "These peppers aren't hot, are they?" because such a question is guaranteed to get the answer "no," as the shopper has expressed a clear preference. It's far safer to ask in a way that prevents the vendor from guessing the answer you want, such as "Are these hot or not?"

The Turks are extremely proud of their nation, its past and, in the case of secular Turks, Atatürk's reforms. They will want to take you to historical sites and also to modern facilities to show you that Turkey has all the amenities available in Europe. Visitors should be careful in making comparisons because people can be sensitive to criticism. If you remember the Turkish worldview, its core values of shame, honor, loyalty, and unity, you will recognize the patterns of deeper meaning behind your hosts' behavior.

Turkish people often feel personally responsible for the success of a visitor's stay. They do not want you to be disappointed and as such may plan a series of outings for you. If they feel that you are not enjoying yourself, they may well redouble their efforts to ensure that you have a good experience—so be sure to let your hosts know that you are having a good time!

GREETINGS

Introductions and greetings are very important in Turkey, and there are formalities to follow. Generally, people greet each other with a kiss on both cheeks, man to man or woman to woman. This is common in a business context, too, if there is a long-standing relationship between the two parties. An appropriate greeting from man to woman is either a nod or a "dead fish" handshake with as little contact as possible if you do not know each other well. Sometimes, as a sign of respect for the elderly, younger people may kiss the hand and press it to their forehead.

When you are introduced to someone for the first time, you should reply "*Memnun oldum*" ("Pleased to meet you"). When entering someone's home, or a meeting room, or joining a restaurant table full of people, it's important to go around and greet everyone present, not just the people you know, and perhaps shake the hand of each person. If an elderly person arrives after you, it is polite to stand up for him or her. The same is true for a more senior person in a business context. The greeting itself is important, and certain key phrases need to be learned. As you enter, individuals will say "*Hoş geldiniz!*" ("Welcome!"). You should reply "*Hoş bulduk!*" ("Glad to be here!"). If your friend is religious, they are more likely to greet you with "*Selam aleyküm*" ("May God's peace be with you"); the reply to this is "*Aleyküm selam*" ("And also with you").

ATTITUDES TOWARD FOREIGNERS

As mentioned, Turkish people are hospitable and courteous, and this extends to strangers too. A visitor is called "*Tanrı misafiri,*" meaning "God's guest," implying that they should be looked after as if they had been sent to you as an envoy from God. There are other Turkish proverbs that reflect this attitude too, such as: "A guest comes with ten blessings, eats one and leaves nine," and "The master of the house is the servant of the guest." As such, being someone's guest in Turkey means that you will be treated very well indeed.

Wealthier people in Turkey will have traveled and may even have lived abroad for education or work. Most others will have formed their view of foreigners through Hollywood films, foreign serials shown on TV or on Netflix, and by meeting tourists. This means that many will have a rather selective view of what life is like abroad, and what foreigners themselves are like. Some Turks have the impression that the streets of

Europe and America are paved with gold and may find it hard to understand why someone with a sought-after foreign passport might want to move to Turkey.

In general, Europeans and Americans are considered to be well educated, to have good business ethics, and to be strong in areas such as planning ahead. However, they are also considered to display negative qualities such as individualism and competitiveness, and to be distant or cold.

In business, for example, Turkish companies are eager to work with foreign firms as foreigners are seen as bringing know-how, in the form of either management practice or specialist knowledge, while a Turkish partner provides expertise in distribution, familiarity with the local regulations, and a network of local contacts. Indeed, some of the most successful companies in Turkey are such joint ventures.

However, some ultra-nationalists believe that there should be no need for foreign goods or foreign-run companies in Turkey and, when a problem arises, you may notice that the blame is often shifted on to "foreign provocation."

JOINING CLUBS

There are many clubs and associations that people can join to meet new people, both locals and expats alike. International clubs represented in Turkey and run by Turks include the Rotary Club and the Lion's

Club, both of which are very active in charitable work. There are also associations in most of the big cities that function as support and social networks for foreigners resident in Turkey, such as the American Women's Association and International Women of Istanbul. Sports and general interest clubs are popular too. Golf courses and country clubs are less common and more exclusive. If you have a particular interest, both Facebook and Instagram are excellent resources for seeing what's available locally and for making first contact.

INVITATIONS HOME

Turks are wonderful hosts. When invited, you should always try to accept as it's rude not to. There are various customs associated with being a guest in Turkey that you should be aware of. In any situation though, if you are unsure, you can watch what the others do, and do the same. For example, if you see that shoes have been removed at the door, you should too. In this case, slippers will be provided.

When you arrive, a little refreshing cologne will be poured into your cupped hands. Wipe your hands together and rub the back of your neck with it.

Two or three generations may live under one roof, which can be daunting when you are first introduced, but remember to greet everyone in the room. If you are sitting down when new guests arrive, stand up to greet them.

Your hostess will ensure that everyone is comfortable. An evening meal may start late; the usual time being about 8:00 p.m. You are not expected to arrive exactly at the mealtime—usually you will be invited earlier, so that you can sit and talk with your hosts first.

During the meal, your hostess will want to look after you and will offer to serve you each dish. You shouldn't serve yourself. At this point it is customary to say the phrase "*Afiyet olsun!*" ("*Bon appetit*") to each other at the table. You can compliment the person who cooked the food by saying "*Elinize sağlık,*" which means "Health to your hands." When you've eaten everything on your plate, your hostess will offer you more. It is important for Turkish hosts to be sure that they have done their best for you in serving you a large and wonderful meal, so even if you refuse, she may press you several times to have an extra helping. If you are full you can refuse, complimenting her on the food; placing your right-hand palm down on your chest is a polite way of both expressing gratitude for the food and showing that you are full and do not want more. Depending on the situation, the hostess may not sit with you at the table. If your hosts have children, don't be surprised at how late they might stay up.

When dinner is over, even though it may seem late, you shouldn't leave right away as enjoying each other's company after the meal is important. Then, when the evening seems to have come to an end, don't just get up and say you have to go. Start the process gently by dropping a few hints that you will need to leave soon.

You are asking permission to leave. A short time later you should mention it again. Your host will try to encourage you to stay longer. When you are preparing to leave, they will insist on helping you with your coat. Your shoes should be put on in the hallway by the door or outside the door in the building.

As a guest you are entitled to respect. You are in a special category and will be treated and served well. Your host will expect to put on a spread (if not, they will feel they have been rude)—a potluck supper is definitely not Turkish! Even if you're dropping in for coffee your host will produce a range of both sweet and savory food to accompany it. The visitor should realize that if an offer is extended to stop by any time, it is truly meant and taken literally and your Turkish friend will be offended if you wait for an invitation for a definite time. Conversely, your Turkish friend may call on you when you least expect it.

GIFT GIVING

When visiting someone in their home, take a small gift such as flowers or chocolate. The gift should always be wrapped, in wrapping paper or even in a plastic bag. Your hostess will probably not open it in front of you.

Be careful not to compliment your host on something or it may be given to you as a gift. Appreciating a picture or vase or other possession may be taken as a request for it to be given to you.

It is quite usual for people to offer neighbors some food if they have had a baking day, and some may even drop round with food to welcome you to the apartment when you move in. If your neighbor gives you a plate of food you should accept it, but don't return the plate empty. Fill it with some food of your own.

ETIQUETTE

In social settings, age is respected. Turks will show deference to an older person by giving them the most comfortable seat, allowing them to choose the music or TV program, and listening to their opinions without disagreeing.

It is considered extremely rude in Turkey to interrupt someone who is speaking, even if they are wrong. Listening is a sign of respect. Looking bored, looking away or at paperwork while someone is talking is rude—it doesn't only show disrespect, it also dishonors the speaker in front of all the others present.

In conversation, it may sometimes be wiser not to give your opinion but just to nod to indicate that you are listening. Even though things may not be what you are used to, it is impolite to criticize Turkey, your elders, or of course your hosts. If you have a different opinion, or disagree in a social context, it is often best to say nothing—as a guest you shouldn't take it upon yourself to try to correct an accepted historical view. To the same extent, certain political issues, such as Kurds and Armenians, should be avoided.

CHAPTER FIVE

AT HOME

Turkish social structure is a fusion of the Ottoman Empire's Islamic values and the modern Republic's secular values. For the most part a mutual synthesis of these two different, even antagonistic, cultures has been achieved. Only recently has Turkey become more polarized, and today, cultural differences between the two poles are more evident.

The population movement from rural to urban areas over the past half century has been significant and has brought about major changes in the family structure.

THE FAMILY

The importance of the family can be seen in the fact that the Turkish language has a special vocabulary for family relationships. For example, specific words indicate whether a person belongs to the husband's or the wife's side of the family, or is an older or younger sibling.

Generally speaking, especially among poorer, less educated, or more religious people, men will be honored before women, and a sister will defer to a brother, even if he is younger.

Family members are expected to look after the weak and elderly. A household normally consists of a married couple and their children, and may well include elderly parents and unmarried brothers or sisters.

Regardless of where family members live, they all have particular responsibilities and together serve the common good of the family. This includes physical protection, economic support, and upholding the reputation of the family.

Though individualism is becoming more prevalent among some, Turkey is still very much a consensus- and group-based society, where each person has a responsibility to others in the group, a concept well illustrated by the local proverb, "Look after the orphan, feed the hungry, separate the fighters in a quarrel." One practical example of this outlook is that people do not want to make decisions on an individual basis, even on the smallest thing. Ask a group of Turks what they would like to eat and most will hesitate to make suggestions. They each want to say what they think the others want to hear. That said, Turks are open to new ideas—as long as those ideas do not interfere with group solidarity.

Terraced houses in Istanbul.

LIVING CONDITIONS

Most housing in Turkey, especially in urban areas, consists of apartment complexes. More recently, a number of gated communities have been built and are popular. For most Turks, living close to one's family is considered important when choosing where to live, and often extended families will purchase separate apartments in the same building. A large percentage of the population rent rather than own their apartment and, as the population continues to increase (though at a slower rate than in the past), houses all over Turkey are gradually being knocked down and apartment complexes built in their place.

In rural Turkey, it is common for farmers to live in the village and commute daily to the fields to work, rather than living in isolated farmhouses as is often the case in America and Europe.

As we previously discussed, in Turkey much importance is placed on making a good impression on visitors. To that end, a formal room is always kept very clean and tidy for entertaining guests who may drop in or who are invited, with furnishings covered when not in use. There is usually a second room for use by the family.

Balconies are important and serve as a place for entertainment and relaxation. In long summer evenings the family may eat on the balcony and sit talking and relaxing in the night air. A more recent trend in new buildings is to have closed balconies that are kept cool with air conditioning.

In general, there is a strong sense of neighborliness; newcomers are often welcomed to the building, and wives will often meet during the day for tea parties, rotating from house to house each week. Some apartment buildings have a janitor, or *kapıcı*, who acts as caretaker and does small jobs for the tenants such as daily shopping for bread and taking out the trash. In gated communities, the security guards often provide similar services. In both cases, salaries are covered by a monthly service charge paid by each dwelling.

Furnishings and Appliances
In villages furnishing can be very basic, consisting of a carpet, couch and/or cushions to sit on around the wall. The room will have a large cupboard and china cabinet for storage. Every house will have a large TV and often many cell phones too. In the city, the style will be more

Western. The formal living room will have a fashionable suite and lovely rugs. Since the early 1980s electrical appliances have been easily available in Turkey and most homes will be very well equipped.

DAILY LIFE AND ROUTINE

Turkish society is undergoing a radical transformation. There has been considerable progress toward raising the status of women in terms of autonomy and rights, and women are achieving greater independence through higher levels of education and employment.

Traditionally, in daily life men deal with the world outside the family. They are considered the protectors and women are expected to submit to their authority. Meanwhile, the role of women is to care for the family and the home. Modern Turks jokingly describe these roles as "Minister of State" and "Minister of Foreign Affairs."

In rural areas, a woman's world is often her children, household, and pride in domestic skills. In urban areas and among the middle and upper classes, however, women are more active in the public realm and take pride in both their home and their work. The cost of living in the large cities, particularly if families want to provide their children with private education and other opportunities, means that more Turkish women are going out to work. This broadens their horizons, provides a sense of financial independence, and changes their expectations for both themselves and their children.

Overall, educated middle-class women have more say in decision-making, choice of spouse, and size of family, and more economic independence and involvement in public life. Women who exhibit maturity and wisdom are today well respected in the public sector.

The honor of the family is reflected in its outward appearance and to this end, home and public areas are kept very clean. Windows are ritually washed at least once a week, sometimes every day. Generally, men and male children do not help around the house.

Modern Turkish women may do their weekly shopping at the supermarket, but they will make a point of going to the weekly bazaar to buy fresh fruit and vegetables. These bazaars are set up in different areas of the city on different days, and a number of residential roads are closed for the bazaar stalls and awnings to be set up. For daily needs, on nearly every corner there is a small grocer called a *bakkal*. These are facing fierce competition from discount supermarket chains that have spread to every busy street. If you live in a building with a grocer on the ground floor, there is an efficient system of lowering a basket on a long rope from the window, with a note in it with your shopping list. The grocer puts the items in the basket and you pull the basket up. Shopping done!

In recent years, Internet grocery shopping has become extremely popular and today most supermarket chains handle online orders. Meanwhile,

Despite an abundance of supermarkets, many still prefer to buy their fresh fruit and vegetables at the bazaar.

companies like Getir, which was founded in Istanbul in 2015 and has since expanded to the USA and much of Western Europe, ensure that necessities can be delivered quickly.

URBAN LIFE

Turkey's cities are sophisticated centers with full amenities while rapid urbanization has seen both sweeping demographic changes and developmental challenges emerge.

Metropolitan centers are often encircled by slum dwellings called *gecekondu*, which translates as "built during the night." These slums were originally created by newly arrived migrants, many of whom have now lived in them for years. When they first arrived they usually built four simple walls with a roof. Then, as money becomes available, another floor is added and more relatives from the village can come to live. Gradually the local authorities connect gas, electricity, and water services to these areas, and build roads. Today, many of these areas are gradually being bulldozed and replaced with new roads and high-rise buildings; sometimes these are expensive private complexes, and sometimes government-sponsored affordable housing.

RURAL LIFE

Village life is hard, and poverty is widespread. Rural areas are also more conservative in their values, and superstitious. As previously described, it is largely a world controlled by men, where much of the hard labor both in and out of the home is done by women. It is also typically feudal. The landowners control the villages and regions, and many of the farms are owned by one wealthy man who hires the workers.

In terms of produce, Turkey is fairly self-sufficient and also exports to neighboring countries. While the rural areas are poor and their production lacks technology, they have real potential for agricultural development and growth, hindered mainly by mismanagement and fear of upsetting the powerful rural elite.

Rural families tend to have many children and often, when those children come of age, they migrate to a city where more work and educational opportunities are available. A Turk's link with their home village is lifelong, however (see the concept of *memleket* on page 75 for more).

Each village is a close-knit society and in general, villagers are generously hospitable to outsiders. If visiting a village, because of transportation schedules it may be necessary to stay overnight. It is the guest's choice to stay as long as he or she wants, and a good host will not ask, "How long are you staying?"

CHILDREN

Turks love children. Adults pinch the cheeks of a child to let them know that they are loved, people stop to watch a child go by, and even macho teenage boys will fuss over a baby.

Generally speaking, in Turkey children are not held to a strict routine. They stay up late and, rather than hiring a babysitter so that mom and dad can go out alone, are usually taken everywhere. Children are welcome in most venues, including smart restaurants and hotels, and they are not much reprimanded as it is believed that children should not be disciplined for what they cannot understand. Even older children are unlikely to be disciplined in public. Older children help with their younger siblings and often the *abla* (eldest sister) is eager to be given special responsibility to help with the younger children.

In Turkish cities, it is expensive to raise children; the trend for middle-class families who wish to give their children a private education and other advantages is to have just one child or to have a relatively large age gap between children. In order to counter the country's dwindling population growth, President Erdoğan has publicly, and somewhat controversially, encouraged families to have at least three children.

CHANGING LIFESTYLES

Turkey has become a consumer society, and this has been accompanied by rising expectations. Over the past decade it has enjoyed an economic boom that has benefited not only the secular urban elites, but also the conservative supporters of the AKP governing party and former rural entrepreneurs. Their upward mobility has led to the formation of an Islamic, urban middle class.

This new Islamic bourgeoisie has money to spend, and the opportunities to do so are increasingly diverse: luxury gated communities, restaurants, and hotels catering to a more pious lifestyle are springing up in urban centers.

In the cities, modernization and industrialization have resulted in a shift away from Turkey's traditional, male-dominated society to consumer-led egalitarianism. Not that long ago it was rare to see women in certain parts of town buying electrical goods, as these were male preserves. Today such goods are available in large, brightly lit shopping malls that are packed with shoppers in the evenings and on weekends.

Lifestyle differences vary with the level of industrialization. Family authority patterns are being affected. Greater educational opportunities mean that younger members of a family may quite easily earn more than their parents. Turks in their fifties grew up at a time when there were many shortages; they want their children and grandchildren to have all the opportunities they missed and this often results in children being materialistically focused.

Now that some women work outside the home, children may go to nurseries or kindergartens. In the cities, family units may be smaller, as young couples become more mobile and live further away from their relatives. Because of this, fewer relatives may live in the same building, and as strangers move in Turks may complain that there is less neighborliness than there used to be.

Fashion
People in urban areas are very fashion-conscious. Turks always look stylish when they go out and when they receive guests. It is part of one's honor and self-respect to be well dressed and importance is placed on designer labels.

A large part of a working woman's salary is spent on clothing and cosmetics. It would be considered shameful for her to go out not looking her best. Conservative Muslim women are also fashion-conscious and within specific parameters, fashion sense finds expression. For example, there are "rules" governing the make, design, and tying of your headscarf, and many women wear designer jeans under their long raincoats and robes.

Across society, clean shoes matter and where possible, are kept polished and shining. If you have walked in a muddy street, wipe your shoes with a cloth before entering a building. When wearing sandals, toenails should be neat and clean. Turkish women love to have manicures and pedicures.

Turks are becoming more aware of the importance of good health and staying in shape. A daily walk or jog is routine for many, both young and old, while gyms and beauty salons have become ubiquitous.

RITES OF PASSAGE

Births

Turks, we have seen, are very family oriented. The country's birth rate has dropped in recent decades, and today urban families increasingly choose to have only one or two children, and to give birth at a hospital. Private hospitals offer the most modern technology, advice, and good prenatal care. These women tend to prefer a caesarean birth. Rural women tend to give birth at home with a midwife.

In villages it is traditional for the grandparents to choose the baby's name, while in cities it is the parents who choose. Some urban families like to keep the tradition, however, by having another name added by elderly relatives, which usually precedes the parents' name in order, and in daily life, Turks will use the second of two names. For example, Mehmet Cenk Atakan would be known as Cenk Atakan or M. Cenk Atakan, where Cenk may be chosen by the parents, and Mehmet by an elderly relative. There may be a religious ceremony for naming the baby, involving an imam coming to the home and reciting from the Koran. The imam then whispers into the baby's ear, "Your name is . . ." The ceremony ends with a blessing on the household.

In urban areas children of either sex are valued, although sons are preferred. In villages a son is considered more valuable because he brings growth to the family through marriage, whereas the daughter will grow up, marry, and leave. (If there is a lull in conversation and everyone falls silent, someone may say "A daughter has been born"—that is, something has happened to put a damper on the party!) A family member may shoot a rifle into the air to celebrate a birth.

The child is then registered as belonging to the extended family of the father. The registration involves much detail. Each family has a number that is representative of the wider clan, rather than just the small family unit, and the child will be allocated an ordinal number showing its position in the clan (number one was the oldest person back in the Atatürk era).

It is usual for friends and family to visit the mother and baby as soon as possible after the birth, and bring gifts for the baby. Turks tend not to buy much before the birth, for fear of tempting fate. It is customary for the mother and baby to not go out for the first forty days.

Circumcision

Circumcision is a rite of passage for a boy and signifies his becoming a man. It is also one of the signs of being a Muslim, though circumcision is practiced by Jews too. Among Muslim Turks, the son is usually circumcised around the age of eight, but some families may have two sons circumcised at the same time because of the expense of separate parties. The circumcision party involves the boy wearing a special suit for a week before, just like a little sultan with his sequined cape, hat, and scepter.

A popular custom is to parade the child around town in a convoy of cars, with much honking of

Celebrations mark the circumcision ceremony.

horns. Religious families have a recital of a poem about Muhammad just before the circumcision. The actual ceremony is usually performed in public on a white bed. The child receives a lot of presents—often toy guns and the like. A wealthy businessman may show his benevolence by paying for the requisite party for poor boys in the neighborhood, or for the sons of his employees.

National Service

The phrase "*En büyük asker bizim asker*"—"The greatest soldier is our soldier"—is very popular. After age eighteen, every man has to do six months of military service, though it can be deferred if he is in full-time education. Every so often the government offers the option of paying a large sum and doing just one month. Over the last few decades, problems in the southeast have discouraged individuals from signing up for fear of being sent there as part of their service.

When a young man leaves for military service, his friends give him a big send-off. This moment is another significant rite of passage and when older men get together it is common for national service stories to be shared.

All enlistees have one month of training, and assignments are then made based on education and skill level. The better educated get office jobs and other strategic appointments. The army reinforces national unity and promotes the strong secular teaching that upholds the Republic. Also, it often helps village youths to improve their reading and social skills.

Every Turkish male is theoretically part of the army reserve and can be called up in a time of war.

Marriage

When it comes to socializing, young people mostly go out in a group and couples tend not to go out in public without a chaperon. Spending time alone together is seen as extremely loose and endangers the girl's reputation.

An interesting development in recent years has been the introduction of dating apps, which are available and used in Turkey. The strong desire in many parts of society for family approval and indeed involvement in the choice of spouse means that these apps are often viewed with suspicion by the more traditional. However, those with a more secular or independent outlook on life and love can be found using the same popular apps that are used abroad.

Marriage generally involves the family and its approval to some degree. Arranged marriages still take place in villages, or among the very wealthy, where there may be an alliance of interests. Often the groom will be considerably older than the bride because he has completed military service and has had to work to earn some money before considering marriage. All that said, marrying for love is becoming more common among young middle-class urban Turks, and they sometimes do so without parental consent.

The bride and her family will have been preparing a *çeyiz* (dowry), which includes clothing and household goods. This is kept for the daughter until a marriage date has been set. When a couple decides to get married there are certain steps that must be taken: *sözlü*, *nişanlı*, and *evli*.

Sözlü is a pre-engagement arrangement. This officially sanctions the couple seeing each other and spending time together, although not yet alone.

It is a serious commitment, and it is considered a grave breach of honor to break it.

Nişanlı means "engaged." The process of becoming engaged involves all members of both families. The hopeful bridegroom's family goes to the woman's family to ask for her hand in marriage. This is a formal visit; they will be wearing their best clothes and will be given the best refreshments. In order for the man not to lose face, his prospective bride answers his proposal in a subtle way. She makes coffee, and if she wishes to accept the proposal (or is instructed to do so by her mother) she puts sugar in his cup. If she rejects it, she puts salt in the cup.

A party is given to celebrate the engagement, overseen by the family elder. In a ceremony two rings tied to the ends of a ribbon are presented to the groom- and bride-to-be: each puts a ring on their finger and the elder cuts the ribbon.

Evli means "married." The first part of the marriage celebration is the *kına gecesi* (henna party). This is a party given for the bride by a few close friends, a married sister, or the older female relatives. It is a major event in the village. At a certain stage in the evening the single girls will walk in a circle around the bride, carrying candles and handkerchiefs containing henna.

Relatives circle the bride as part of the *kına gecesi*, or henna party.

The bride is then encouraged to open her hand by the mother-in-law offering her a coin. She and her friends will place the henna on their hands. They dance and sing sad songs about losing their friend to another village, and married friends will tell all sorts of horror stories about mothers-in-law.

The official wedding ceremony is civil. The couple obtains a license to marry from the local authority, and an official conducts the ceremony, which is relatively short. If held in a registry office, it is a little like a conveyor belt, so wealthy families prefer to pay to perform the ceremony at home or in a hotel.

A religious wedding is possible, but it is a criminal offense to conduct it before the civil ceremony. It is also an offense to have more than one wife.

During the ceremony, right from the moment when the bride and groom come in, there is a lot of applause. People applaud when "yes" is said and upon the announcement that the couple are married. The bride and groom also try to step on each other's feet. It is believed this will show who will rule the house during the marriage!

Large bouquets of flowers are sent, many photographs are taken, and videos are made. It is customary to give money, gold, and bracelets, and some, usually among less affluent sections of society, make a large demonstration of this. Those giving money pin it on to the bride's dress or the groom's collar.

There is a wedding party afterward, which varies in degree according to circumstances. Every guest is given a little souvenir—a piece of candy, such as a sugarcoated almond, or a small present.

After the couple is married, they need to get a family identity card. The bride is removed from the register of her old family and added to that of her husband. Usually new couples move into fully furnished apartments. Traditionally, their parents are allotted certain rooms to furnish in full.

Dealing With Illness

In traditional Turkish culture, health is considered to be a blessing from God. It is always polite to ask about the health of other people and their family. Turks may believe that an illness is a result of God's punishment, retribution for doing wrong, worry, being the victim of maliciously intended magic, or offending or harming a jinn (evil spirit), in addition to the usual medical explanations.

Sickness is dealt with in many ways. A proverb from eastern Turkey says, "When God gave a problem, he also gave the remedy." Traditional as well as Western medical treatment may be used. Turkish hospitals and medical practitioners are as good as any in Europe, yet most housewives have their own set of recommended cures. Yogurt is considered good for stomach problems, while tying a scarf tightly around one's forehead is believed to help with headaches.

For the religious and superstitious, amulets or armbands bearing verses from the Koran are sometimes used while the shrines of certain saints are also thought to have healing powers. People will travel great distances to visit a shrine or special spa where it is believed the place or the water may cure their ills.

Funerals

Death is generally considered to be the will of God. This does not mean that grief and emotion are at all lessened. When people refer to a deceased person they will often add the adjective *rahmetli* (with the mercy of God) to the person's name.

A visit to the deceased's family is appropriate. Turks will drop everything to run to the side of friends or family who have suffered a loss. There are certain phrases that are polite to say to the bereaved, such as "*Başınız sağolsun*" ("Health to your head"), "*Allah rahmet eylesin*" ("May God grant them mercy"), and "*Allah sabır versin*" ("May God give you patience").

Traditionally, the body should be buried within twenty-four hours. At the service the Fatiha, the first chapter of the Koran, is recited. Praise is offered to Allah, and then a petition for his mercy on the souls of all present and on the soul of the deceased.

Then follows the most important communal act: the discharge. The imam asks, "What was the deceased person like to you?" The reply is "We found him/her to be a good person." The imam asks, "Do you forgive them anything they have done?" The reply is "We forgive them." This is your "final duty" to the deceased, and it is very important to attend the funeral and give them this absolution.

The crowd carries the coffin to the hearse. Burials are in municipal cemeteries, which are planted with cypress trees. The body is buried intact as Muslims believe in bodily resurrection at judgment day. It is taken out of the coffin and buried in its shroud.

The last respectful act is a prayer: "O servant of God, say that my god is Allah, and my prophet is Muhammad, and my book is the Koran, and my religion is Islam."

Rather than sending wreaths and flowers, in Turkey donations are made to charity. At the mosque different charities have stands for donations, or a gift may be sent directly to the charity in memory of the deceased.

It is customary to have a religious ceremony seven days after death and again forty days later, in which the Koran will be read in the home. It is also tradition to distribute a piece of *lokma*, a sweet pastry, at the end of the ceremony. This is done in memory of the deceased. The family will regularly go to the graveside to pray; the deceased are to be visited, greeted, and remembered in prayer.

CHAPTER SIX

TIME OUT

When Atatürk established the Republic of Turkey, he changed the day of rest from the Islamic Friday to Sunday. Thus, the working week runs from Monday to Friday for banks and offices, and from Monday to Saturday for shops. Lots of shops and restaurants are open on Sunday too, though. Religious people may take a long lunch break on Friday to go to the mosque for the holiest prayer service of the week; a small business owner may close his shop or business during this Friday lunch period.

The concept of a "work-life balance" is not a familiar one to most Turks, who often work long hours and often for little financial reward. Working overtime is common, as is rush hour traffic in most major cities, meaning that many are out of home for twelve hours on any given workday. Though the official age of retirement in Turkey is lower than in much of Europe—it is currently sixty for men and fifty-eight for women—it is not uncommon to work beyond this.

What leisure time remains, Turks make the most of, often with their family and friends, socializing and pursuing group activities. Less time is devoted to individual leisure pursuits and hobbies. Turks love to window-shop in the winter and be outside in the summer, and enjoy strolling in parks and on the beach. Meals are shared at restaurants, and hours are whiled away chatting over coffee or tea in a café.

FOOD AND DRINK

Turkish cuisine is one of the many local joys that visitors have to look forward to. There are luscious fruits and vegetables in season, stuffed with rice, raisins, pine nuts, or meat, nourishing stews, and on the coasts, freshly cooked fish straight from the sea.

Turkish cooks are as concerned with presentation as with flavor. A Turkish saying reads "First appeal to the eyes, then fill the stomach."

Lamb is the most popular meat. Beef, often grilled as a kebab, is common, as is chicken. Meat is prepared according to Islamic (Halal) rules, which prohibit the eating of pork, ham, bacon, and other pig products. You may find them at an exclusive restaurant or five-star hotel, but they are not widely available in Turkey.

Rice is usually served, sometimes with currants, pine nuts, and spices. Much fresh produce is home grown. Garlic and olives are used widely, as with much Mediterranean cuisine. Food tends to be seasonal, due to the emphasis on fresh ingredients.

A chef prepares *döner* kebab, a fast-food favorite in Turkey.

Eating Out

Turks are passionate about food. Snacks can be purchased everywhere; sellers roam the streets carrying a flat board loaded with tasty wares on their head. Buffets and kiosks line the roadside, and glass-sided pushcarts display other savories. Commonly enjoyed snacks are nuts and sunflower seeds, sweetcorn, *simit* (sesame-coated bread rings), *kokoreç* (grilled sheep's intestine), fresh fish sandwiches, fried mussels on a stick, and meatballs.

Late nights are common, and Turks thoroughly enjoy going out on the town, as families, in groups, or on their own. There are restaurants and cafés to satisfy every palate, from regional fish to meat, pastry shops to delicatessens, and even sushi bars in trendy urban areas. Turks generally have supper around 7:30 or 8:30 p.m.

Once seated, you may find that you are not offered a menu. Instead, the waiter will recite the list of fare, or you will find a QR code at your table linking to an online menu. Don't be shy when it comes to choosing your food in Turkey; you can often inspect the kitchen, ask questions, and point to what you want. There are many family-run specialty restaurants as well as major chains such as Sahan, Midpoint, Big Chefs, Cook Shop, and Happy Moons.

It is easy to "eat out at home" too. Most restaurants in Turkey—from McDonald's to the most ethnic cuisine—offer home delivery, although their telephone operators and motorbike delivery boys often won't speak English. The food delivery app Yemeksepeti

("Foodbasket") will enable you to order in English from a variety of local restaurants.

The Turkish dining experience may be one of the most memorable events of your trip. A typical restaurant meal will contain the following courses, with the starters (one cold and one hot) consisting of assorted small dishes on individual plates.

Meze (Cold Starters)

Usually a tray with ten or so varieties will be shown to you to choose from. Typical selections include stuffed vine leaves or green peppers (*dolma*), cheese, vegetables such as eggplant or okra in olive oil, spicy

Popular dishes including (from left to right) *lahmacun*, stuffed vine leaves, bulgur wheat salad, flatbread, and *pide*.

tomato paste, eggplant and watercress folded in garlic yogurt, chickpea paste (hummus), potato salad, and cracked wheat in tomato and chili sauce (*kısır*). There is also usually delicious fresh bread.

Salata (Salad)

Fresh fruit and vegetables are wonderful in Turkey. The two most common types of salad are a "shepherd's salad" (*çoban salatası*) of chopped tomatoes, cucumbers, and onions, and a "seasonal salad" (*mevsim salatası*) of lettuce, grated carrots or red cabbage, tomato and cucumber slices, sweetcorn, and green peppers.

Çorba (Soup)

You must taste red lentil soup (*mercimek*), yogurt and rice soup (*yayla*), or tomato (*domates*), chicken (*tavuk*), or mushroom (*mantar*) soups. Tripe soup (*işkembe*) has a strong smell and is an acquired taste. Soups are often enhanced by freshly squeezed lemon or sweet red pepper fried in butter.

Ara Sıcak (Hot Starters)

Here you can choose from such delights as deep-fried cheese pastry roll (*sigara böreği*), deep-fried balls of rice, mince, and nuts (*içli köfte*), calamari (*kalamar*), and fried mussels (*midye*).

Et (Meat Dishes)

Kebab means "small pieces of meat." "Shish kebab" (*şiş*) is pieces of meat roasted on a skewer. A *döner*

Köfte kebab.

(literally meaning "it turns") is lamb or chicken grilled on a rotating spit. *Döner* kebab is slices of this meat served in bread as a sandwich (*ekmek arası*), wrapped in thin pastry (*dürüm*), or on a plate with vegetables. *Köfte* is meatballs made from ground meat, parsley, and bread or rice. Steaks are available, but Turks normally like them well done. "Rare" in Turkey normally corresponds to "medium" elsewhere. Chicken can be found in most preparations, even as a schnitzel. There are various dishes special to regions of Turkey. *İskender kebabı* is slices of lamb served with tomato sauce and yogurt; Adana kebabs are not spicy, but Urfa kebabs are. Other specialty meat dishes to look for are *sarma beyti*, chunks of meat wrapped with thin pastry, and *babaganuş*, chunks of meat served on a bed of eggplant pureed with garlic and lemon.

Balık (Fish)

Fish is best eaten fresh at coastal or lakeside restaurants. It is normally steamed (*buharlı*), grilled (*tava*), or fried (*kızartma*). Popular choices, depending on the time of year, include anchovy (*hamsi*), sea bass (*levrek*), blue fish (*lüfer*), bream (*çipura*), turbot (*kalkan*), and mackerel (*uskumru*). It is a good idea to ask the waiter which fish is freshest and in season.

Pide (Turkish Pizza)

Unlike its Italian cousin, Turkish *pide* does not have tomato sauce, nor is it round but rather long and rolled at the edges. The soft pastry base is topped with white or cheddar cheese, and then, if you wish, meat, spinach, or egg. *Lahmacun* is a special variety of ground meat with tomato and onion sauce on a very thin pastry base. It is rolled and eaten with parsley or chopped lettuce inside.

Tatlı (Dessert)

Turkish dessert is usually very sticky. Try filo pastry soaked in syrup and sprinkled with nuts (*baklava*), a similar dish made with shredded wheat (*kadayıf*), quince in syrup (*ayva tatlısı*), or pumpkin in syrup (*kabak tatlısı*). Alternatives to syrupy desserts are milk pudding (*muhalebe*) or rice pudding (*sütlaç*). Turkish delight (*lokum*) made from rose water,

Sweet and syrupy pistachio *baklava*.

pistachios, coconut, and powdered sugar is eaten as a
dessert or with coffee. It travels well and makes a great
gift item.

Special Diets

With the vast range of fresh fruit and vegetables
available, as well as dishes involving pasta, lentils, and
beans, a vegetarian can find much to eat in Turkey. In
a restaurant if you ask for "no meat" they are likely to
offer you a chicken dish instead, as Turks consider
meat to be red meat. Rather, say *"vejeteryan."*

Vegan, lactose-free, and gluten-free fare is more
difficult to find. Your best choice when eating out
is simply to avoid dishes that will not suit you. In
upmarket bakeries and pastry shops, you may find
some gluten-free bread and cakes. Supermarkets in
more wealthy areas often have "free-from" aisles where

you can buy soy or almond milk and gluten-free flours, breads, cookies, and cakes.

Regional Specialties

Turkish food varies from region to region. Some specialties can be traced back to the nomadic tribesmen of Central Asia: for example, *sucuk* and *pastırma* are forms of spicy cured meat, originally made by putting the meat under the saddle. Pressure from the weight of the rider and salt from the horse's sweat would preserve it.

The southeast has a spicier diet. When urban Turks are on a journey they will stop and buy foods special to each town: for example, Susurluk *ayran* (yogurt drink), Bursa candied chestnuts and peaches, Black Sea hazelnuts and fresh anchovies, Izmit *pişmaniye* (spun sugar), Antep pistachios, and Afyon spicy sausage.

Drinking

Restaurants may or may not serve alcohol, depending on their ownership, the neighborhood they are in, and their proximity to schools. If they do, local (*yerli*) brands are often much cheaper than imported (*ithal*) versions of beer, gin, or wine. Most local alcohol is produced by the state monopoly. Turkish beer is like lager and is served cold. A common brand is Efes (Ephesus) beer, which comes in normal, light, and dark varieties. Turkey has a good range of red and white wines; two of the main vineyards are Doluca and Kavaklıdere. Wine is drunk mainly by the secular middle and upper classes— all alcohol is considered haram and is not permitted by Islam. During Ramadan, out of deference, some

restaurants that would normally serve alcohol will not do so. A law passed in 2013 bans the sale of alcohol after 10:00 p.m. in shops.

Turks love to sit in cafés and chat with their friends. The national alcoholic drink is *rakı*, an aniseed-flavored spirit similar to Greek ouzo that is mixed with water until it turns cloudy. It is also referred to as "lion's milk." The *rakı* table is a ceremonial meal; the *rakı* is drunk with a wide array of hot and cold appetizers.

Strong tea is drunk everywhere and is the universal Turkish offering to guests and friends. It is normally served in a small, tulip-shaped glass with no milk and is usually sweet. It is polite to ask for weak tea if that's your preference, just say "*açık olsun.*" Your glass will be refilled many times. If you don't want any more, place the teaspoon over the top of the glass.

Famous throughout the world, Turkish coffee is drunk in a small cup and is very black and strong. The phrases for describing how you like your coffee are *sade*, no sugar; *az şekerli,* slightly sweetened; *orta*, medium-sweet; and *çok şekerli*, very sweet. Good Turkish coffee is frothy on top. Drink only halfway down, and be careful not to swirl the cup or you will get a mouthful of unpleasant-tasting grounds. A Turkish proverb about friendship and coffee reads "A cup of coffee commits the drinker to forty years of friendship." On a hot day try *ayran*, a refreshing mix of yoghurt and water.

TABLE MANNERS

Table manners vary. The table may be laid by placing the cutlery crossed on the plate. Generally, Turks hold the fork in the right hand and the knife in the left, and do not switch them. There are some strict Muslims who do not use the left hand for eating at all. Turks do not rest a hand on their lap while eating; both hands are kept above the table. When you have finished, place your knife and fork side by side on your plate. Waiters attentively whisk away the empty dishes (hold on to your glass if you are still drinking) and may also remove your plate or cutlery at any time and give you clean ones.

A meal is often part of doing business. If you have been invited, always accept, and don't try to split the cost if your host insists on paying—he would say that you would pay for him if he were in your hometown. If appropriate, you can reciprocate later.

In conservative restaurants, there is usually a family salon and a separate men-only seating area. The old picture of a Turkish restaurant full of cigarette smoke is a thing of the past. Smokers by law now have to sit outside, a change that has led to many restaurants having glassed-in patios to cater for their patrons who wish to smoke.

TIPS (*BAHŞİŞ*)

Employees are often paid the minimum wage and as a result expect tips. Always tip in cash.

Restaurant: 10 percent (not usually added in, unless the menu says so)

Taxi: 10 percent if the ride has been good (typically, round the fare up to the higher TL)

Airport: fixed tariff for baggage (check signs)

Bell boy: US $1–2 per bag. For other tips at a hotel, there is usually a box in reception for all staff: US $5–10

Tour guides: approx. US $2 per person in the group. Same for the driver.

Barber, beauty parlor, Turkish bath: about 10 percent, split between the people who have helped you (it is often acceptable to tuck the money into their pocket).

Car park attendant outside hotel or restaurant: if there is no parking fee and the attendant brings your car to the door, tip US $2–3 (more if yours is a luxury car!)

SHOPPING

From crowded bazaars to high-tech shopping malls, Turkey is a country where you can shop till you drop. Window-shopping is a popular pastime, and many malls, such as Istanbul's İstinye Park, Zorlu Center, and ViaPort feature top European luxury brands. Those visiting from abroad, however, should make sure to experience the colorful and exciting bazaars, the local, open-air markets, and the grand old covered markets where they can find clothing, spices, fresh fruit and vegetables, traditional ceramic wares, rugs, gold, and jewelry.

In bazaars it's usual to bargain; you may end up paying about half the original asking price. When trying out your bargaining skills, it's best to get a rough feel for the real value of the goods before you start, then venture an offer of half that price. Don't start to haggle unless you have a real intention of buying the goods—it's considered very rude to strike a deal through bargaining and then not follow through. Also, specify your method of payment early on. *Nakit* means cash, and you can often get a better deal with it than if you pay with a credit card. Shopping centers and supermarkets have fixed prices so don't try to negotiate there.

Shopping can be an enjoyable social experience, and Turkish women dress well for the occasion. Don't expect to dash into a shop, buy what you need, and dash out: small shopkeepers will offer you tea and expect to chat, particularly in popular tourism spots. Note that even if you get a good deal, your Turkish friends will always say they could have got it for you more cheaply—so why not ask them to come shopping with you? They will enjoy helping you to get a good price.

Bazaars close at sundown but shops in Turkey stay open late into the evening, often until 9:00 or 10:00 p.m. and often seven days a week. There are special neighborhoods for certain goods in each town: there will be a bookshop district, a lighting district, a street with hardware products and so on.

There are many well-respected Turkish and international stores with branches throughout the country, such as Boyner department stores, Carrefour and Migros supermarkets, Beymen, Marks & Spencer, Zara, Mudo, Yargıcı, and more. Reasonably priced jeans and casual clothes can be purchased everywhere from Turkish chains like Colin's, LTB, and LC Waikiki. One upmarket shop of particular interest is Vakko; this family-owned department store sells women's scarves and men's ties made of high-quality silk, featuring designs from Turkish textiles and mosaics or reproductions of contemporary Turkish art.

Leather goods and gold are both very reasonable. Gold is priced by weight; the market price changes daily and is printed in the newspaper just like a currency exchange rate. The vendor will weigh your chosen piece and calculate the price from today's market value. Other great gift items and souvenirs to buy are copper, silverware, and glassware.

Carpets are a must-buy! You'll find a great selection and many different regional designs. They vary in quality, however, and in general, you get what you pay for: the more knots per square centimeter, the more expensive the carpet will be. Some carpets will be made from exquisite silk from the town of Hereke and some from wool, and they will be either machine or handmade. Carpet buying can be a long process, with the owner showing you every carpet in the shop, rolling them out with panache. Don't try to skip this stage: a carpet is not a cheap item, and you are entitled to see the full range. Point out the carpets you like, and these will be set aside for you to look at again later. It is acceptable to try to bargain in this situation and expect to be offered a lot of tea in the process.

People will try to sell you antiques. In particular, boys will approach you as you tour old ruins, offering you little pots or old coins. Be careful because these cannot be taken out of the country legally. There are strict laws governing the export of antiquities and artifacts such as coins, pottery, jewelry, paintings, and carpets.

Tour guides get a commission from the shops they recommend. Take time to look around; cross the street to see a shop that will not be paying your guide a commission and may give you a discount. Also, when meeting Turks in the street in tourist areas, remember that, "My uncle has a good shop" probably means, "I am employed by a particular shopkeeper to approach tourists and take them to his shop." Use your own judgment.

Today shoppers in Turkey have the option of doing much of their shopping online. As far as local retailers are concerned, however, services in English are limited and may require a Turkish credit card for payment.

Trendyol, Hepsiburada, n11, and GittiGidiyor are all popular online shopping platforms locally, and it can often be cheaper to purchase items there than from retailers directly.

CHANGING YOUR MONEY

Credit cards are widely accepted, but you can often get a better deal by paying for things in cash, which you will also need for tips, paying parking assistants, and others. In general, it is better not to exchange much money before traveling to Turkey, as you can often get a better rate there.

Banks are open Mondays to Fridays, though most of them close between 12:30 and 1:30 p.m. for lunch. There are many good Turkish banks, as well as international banks such as HSBC and ING Bank. In recent years Turkey has seen the growth of the *takaful* banking sector, locally called "*katılım,*" or participation banking. As these high street banks are Shariah-compliant, interest is prohibited.

The easiest way to change money is at the *döviz*, a licensed money changer; they are regulated and often give the best rates. Rates will be posted on boards (so compare if two or three *döviz* bureaus are near to each other) and the posted rate is what you get, with no extra commission.

Most hotels will change money, but they give a worse rate than the bank or *döviz*. Beware of money changers on the street. At best you may get a poor rate; at worst you may end up with counterfeit bills.

Credit cards are widely accepted in shops and restaurants. In city stores you are also likely to be able to pay via your cellphone payment app. Visa and Mastercard are widely accepted, American Express less so. Beware of fraud—it's best not to use your card in a small backstreet outfit. Many shops and hotels accept US dollars, euros, and sterling.

MUSIC

Turks love music and those who can afford to go to concerts. A variety of music such as jazz, classical, and pop is available, all with a local twist. Turkish classical music is very distinctive. The rhythm and scale are typically Middle Eastern, and the music is in a choral, folk ballad style. There may be a full choir, or just a solo singer. Typical instruments include the *kanun* (a zitherlike instrument with seventy-two strings), *tambur* (a long-necked stringed instrument similar to the mandolin), *ud* (like a lute), *ney* (a reed flute), and *saz* (a small lute). Turkish music is filled with emotion and expression, which usually gets the audience swaying and singing along. Live entertainment in restaurants includes some traditional folk songs (*fasıl*).

Popular music consists of Western-style Turkish pop. This has a lively rhythm that sets your feet dancing and hips and shoulders swaying but is based

Men playing the *bağlama saz*.

on the Middle Eastern scale. Turks will love it if you know the names of pop legends like Sezen Aksu, Tarkan, or Sertab Erener, whose hit song "Every Way That I Can" was a Eurovision Song Contest winner. More recent stars of the genre include singers like Mustafa Ceceli, Oğuzhan Koç, and Bilal Sonses.

When on buses or in taxis, your driver may well be listening to what Turks call "Arabesque," songs that typically lament the treachery of a loved one, or a case of unrequited love. Influenced by emotive minor-key melodies of the Middle East and Southern Europe, it can't be missed. Icons of the genre include Orhan Gencebay, İbrahim Tatlıses, and Bergen.

CINEMA

Turkish films are very dramatic—the plot nearly always includes gun chases and romance, and they always have a sad ending.

All of the latest Hollywood films are shown at your local cinema. Normally films will be in their original language, with Turkish subtitles. The only exception to this is children's films, which will be dubbed. Halfway through the film, there will be an abrupt break. The film reel has not snapped—this is the mandatory ten-minute break to allow the Turkish cinemagoers to enjoy their cigarettes. Cinemas were closed at various points during the Covid-19 pandemic, but following the widespread rollout of vaccinations reopened with no major restrictions except the need to present a QR code via the government track and trace app HES (HayatEveSığar).

Netflix is extremely popular in Turkey, both for its foreign films and shows, which are dubbed into Turkish or subtitled, as well as for its wide range of Turkish productions, which can also be watched dubbed into English or subtitled. These include shows by popular comedians like Cem Yılmaz, historical dramas such as *Diriliş: Ertuğrul* (*Resurrection: Ertuğrul*), action films and series including *Organize Süçler* (*Organized Crimes*) and *Kurtlar Vadisi* (*Valley of the Wolves*), and dramas like *Atiye* (*The Gift*) and *Kulüp* (*The Club*).

DANCE

In Turkey this encompasses regional folk dances and folklore, classical ballet, and modern dance. *Halay* is a well-known folk dance performed in a circle, accompanied by a drum or pipe.

The belly dance is synonymous with Turkey, although it did not originate there, but elsewhere in the Middle East. The specially trained dancers are called *dansöz*. A dancer may be hired to perform at a private party for a wedding or birthday celebration; others appear regularly as part of a cabaret in a club, or at special shows put on for tourists. Turks of both sexes and all ages appreciate the skill and training of a top dancer, and will show their appreciation of a good dancer by clapping along and tucking a note under her bra strap when she passes their table. She will share this money with the music group. The most fervent admirers of the belly dancers are not always male; even conservatively dressed and seemingly devout women can be found cheering at shows.

HUMOR

The Turks have a good sense of humor and can poke fun at themselves and others. Nasrettin Hoca ("Hodja") and Temel from the Black Sea region are famous characters in jokes. Nasrettin Hoca's jokes are clever stories that expose the shortcomings of society in an ingenuous kind of way. Temel jokes project an image of simple country folk—Temel is always the idiot who makes a major mistake.

Karagöz and Hacivat are shadow puppets, dressed in Ottoman dress. This is a folk art tradition, and is not just for children. Their plays are comic political satire. Karagöz (the village idiot) says the wrong words and gets hold of the wrong end of the stick. Hacivat is bright and always sets him straight. This traditional art form is often updated to poke fun at modern public figures and issues.

SPORTS

The National Game

Turkish men don't just love soccer—they're crazy about it—and every summer streets around the country turn into makeshift soccer pitches. The best teams are Beşiktaş (The Eagles), Istanbul, black and white; Fenerbahçe (The Canaries), Istanbul, navy and yellow; Galatasaray (The Lions), Istanbul, red and yellow (chant: "Cim Bom Bom"); Trabzonspor (The Tigers), Trabzon, maroon and blue.

Turkey has been successful in Europe and the World Cup, and many players have gained renown overseas at foreign clubs. Turks will ask whom you support, and you'll impress them if you know a bit about their teams and famous Turkish players, like Arda Turan of Galatasaray, Cenk Tosun, who currently plays for English Premier League side Everton, and Fenerbahçe midfielder Mesut Özil who, despite being German, is claimed by the Turks as one of their own thanks to his being of Turkish descent. Conversely, you will find football fans in Turkey

to be well informed about European teams. Fans of
local sides are fanatical, and every soccer game is like a
festival, with firecrackers, chants, and drums.

Other Sports

Gyms can be found in all cities, and a chain called B-fit
caters only for women. Indoor swimming pools are
becoming more common but are generally found only in
major hotels and private clubs. Basketball is popular, and
for those who play tennis, courts can be found though
for a fee. Jogging has become more popular in cities.

Skiing is possible during the winter months at
Uludağ near Bursa, Kartalkaya near Bolu, Palandöken
near Erzurum, and Saklıkent in Antalya.

If you like to play golf, there are some country clubs
on the outskirts of Istanbul, and international-standard
golf resorts near Antalya.

Lottery and Gambling

The national lottery is called Milli Piyango, and the
largest jackpots are at New Year and other national
holidays. It seems that nearly everybody buys a ticket
in the hope of winning something. There is a one-in-
five chance that you will win the *amorti* and get your
ticket money back. Instant lottery and a pools system
of gambling on the results of football matches are
also available.

Casino-style gambling was made illegal some years
ago, and all the casinos in Turkey were closed down.
Those who like to indulge fly to Northern Cyprus,
where every major hotel has a large casino attached.

THE HAMAM

Hamam is the Turkish word for the traditional bathhouse. In the past, people did not have baths in their houses, but went to the hamam. In Ottoman times it was the center of gossip and social activity. Nowadays it is mainly used on special occasions (for example, as part of a bride's prenuptial preparations) or by curious tourists.

Men and women have separate sections in the hamam. You will be given the essentials: a large towel (*peştemal*) that you tie around your waist to protect your modesty, special wooden block shoes, and a bowl. You bring your own soap. The bathing room is very steamy. There are sinks around the walls, and a channel of water runs around the perimeter. You choose your spot and sit on the marble floor in front of a sink with hot and cold taps. You fill your bowl and pour the water over yourself. Turks believe that water should be running—to sit in a tub of water is unclean. Part of the experience is to get really clean by exfoliating the top layer of dead skin. For best results don't use soap until you have been exfoliated. Plenty of hot water on the skin means you can rub this layer off with a special sponge, or have a masseur/masseuse do this for you. This can be rough!

In the steam room you wash, and you can have a vigorous massage while lying on a heated slab of marble. The whole bath area has under-floor heating. If you feel it will be your only chance, go for the whole works (the rub with rough gloves, the soaping, and the face and feet massages).

There is a Turkish proverb, "*Hamama giren terler*," "He who goes into a hamam will sweat." If you don't like the heat, get out!

VISITING A MOSQUE

Each neighborhood takes pride in having a beautiful mosque—the spiritual focus of the community. It represents a combination of art and spirituality. The graceful, slender minarets lead the eye heavenward, and the interior, too, provides a feast for the eyes, from the intricate calligraphic designs on the walls to the patterned carpets stretching across the floor.

You may be asked to enter through a separate doorway. Visitors are not allowed during prayer time. Men should not go into the section reserved for women. Be respectful, and cover up; in the mosques frequented by tourists, there are wraps for women with too-short skirts or men with shorts. Women must also cover their heads. Everyone is expected to leave their shoes outside.

CHAPTER SEVEN

TRAVEL, HEALTH, & SAFETY

With its magnificent climate, diverse terrain, and reliable infrastructure, Turkey is a great destination for those who enjoy traveling. Along Aegean and Mediterranean coastlines, there are beautiful beaches and lively nightlife, history buffs will find an amazing range of archaeological ruins, and backpackers can explore beautiful scenery while discovering more remote parts of the country.

There are tourist information offices operated by the Ministry of Tourism in every city, and in Istanbul there are branches at each of the major tourist sites. Here free brochures, maps, and information are available.

ROADS AND DRIVING

Paradoxically, in a country where regulations and bureaucracy mean that things can take a long time,

Turkish drivers are in an amazing hurry. They are risk takers, and often appear aggressive.

While there have been great improvements to the main road network in recent years, heavy traffic, speeding, poor signaling accompanied by risky overtaking, potholes, and unclear signposts generally make driving a challenge. Urban rush hour is not for the fainthearted. Fast jeeps, trucks, old tractors, motorbike delivery boys, and the occasional pedestrian all share the same roads.

Westerners will need to learn a different driving etiquette. The use of the horn is not always negative. It can mean "hurry up," "watch out," "hello," "do you want a lift?" and so on. In Turkey cars drive on the right. Drivers do not always stick to the designated lane and may create a new one, and often turn without signaling. In a Turkish car the indicator light rarely wears out—but the horn is sure to!

Turkish traffic lights have some interesting features. Many have been fitted with a countdown showing how many seconds there are till the light changes. This enables traffic near a green light to speed up to get through just in time before the light changes, or cars stopped at red to rev their engines ready to peel off the second the light changes. The definition of a nanosecond in Turkey is the time it takes between the traffic light turning green and the driver behind hooting because you haven't moved yet. Traffic lights often have no amber, but, curiously, at night they can be switched off and just flash amber.

To survive driving in Turkey you must learn to be assertive. While there are rules for who has the right of way (for example, on a traffic circle, priority is for vehicles joining from the right), this is in practice based on who gets their nose out first. Drivers tend to be impatient and reluctant to back up if another car comes head-on in a narrow street. Traffic rules are flagrantly flouted, but if you get caught you will be fined and will receive penalty points on your license.

On intercity routes, cameras and speed traps with radar are routine. The speed limits are 31 mph (50 kmph) in cities, 56 mph (90 kmph) on open road (62 mph/100 kmph on divided highways), and 75 mph (120 kmph) on expressways.

If you do have an accident, generally whoever hits the other car is at fault, even if it pulled out without looking. So be ready to make an emergency stop at all times, and watch out for motorbikes and electric scooters on the road. If you have an accident, those involved need to complete an insurance report form and swap copies. Photos will help you with your claim. If both sides agree on the cause of the accident you don't need to call the police, unless someone is injured, in which case the cars should not be moved—leaving the scene before the police come is punishable by a fine.

Don't confuse Turkish driving etiquette with your own. The flashing of headlights doesn't mean "You go first." It means "Don't even think about it: I'm going."

The main expressway going from Bulgaria through Istanbul and Ankara (the TEM), the three Istanbul bridges, and the car tunnel under the Bosporus and some other inter-city roads are toll roads. In order to drive on toll roads, drivers must purchase a prepaid HGS tag in the form of sticker or card for electronic identification at toll gates. These can be obtained at certain petrol stations, post office branches, and some banks, and can be topped up as necessary.

Traffic in the big cities can be very heavy, particularly at rush hours. Many drivers in Turkey use Google Maps and Yandex to help them find the quickest route and avoid congestion.

Drinking and Driving

Driving under the influence of alcohol is illegal. There are not many random breath tests, but you will be tested routinely if you are involved in an accident, even if it was not your fault. There are strict penalties also for driving under the influence of alcohol—the legal limit is 0.5 per ml.

Car and Driver's License

Foreigners can drive on a foreign license in Turkey for a period of up to six months, but then you must replace your license with a Turkish one by taking the Turkish driving test.

When purchasing insurance, it is for the car, not the driver. There are two types: *zorunlu trafik* is mandatory and gives low protection; *kasko* is fully comprehensive coverage.

Cars registered to foreigners in Turkey are given special number plates that start with "M". Only the registered owner or members of their family can drive such a vehicle. But foreigners can drive vehicles registered to Turks with no legal or insurance restrictions apart from having an appropriate driving license.

Crossing the Road

Pedestrians need nerves of steel. It is best to cross at traffic lights (many lights have a countdown for pedestrians as well), but still check both ways that all traffic has stopped. Don't be fooled into thinking that black and white stripes on the road mean you have the right of way as a pedestrian. Crossing the street is dangerous. Whenever possible, use a footbridge or underpass (the latter often has nice kiosks and shops).

INTERCITY TRAVEL

Planes

There are currently fifty-eight airports in Turkey, of which twenty-three are international and thirty-five are domestic. Turkey's national carrier, Turkish Airlines (THY), has a good network connecting all the major cities, while other airlines, including low-cost carriers such as Pegasus and Anadolu Jet, cover the whole country.

Flight times range from one hour for Istanbul to Ankara to two hours from Istanbul to Diyarbakır. Some flights require changing planes in Ankara or Istanbul. Passengers should always travel with ID—this can be your passport or some other form of valid photo identification. Prices are reasonable. When buying tickets, be sure to shop around online where good deals are to be found.

Buses

After planes, buses are the next best way to travel around the country if you have time, and before flights became affordable, the road network was the main means of intercity travel in Turkey. You can book a bus ticket online or just turn up at an out-of-town bus station and hop on. Go to the office of the bus company—if you don't know which to choose, you will be sure to be accosted by men trying to get you to use their company!

Travel between Istanbul and Ankara can take as little as four hours, as does traveling between Istanbul and Izmir. Many buses travel at night (for example, seventeen hours for Istanbul to Trabzon, ten hours for Istanbul to Cappadocia). Some companies have a better safety record than others: Kamil Koç, Ulusoy, and Varan are regarded as the best. On most routes, onboard toilets and meals are provided. On other routes there will be regular stops at service stations or bus stations. Wi-Fi on board is also pretty standard these days. Buses are nonsmoking.

Trains

Train is a popular means of travel in Turkey and, since 2014, has become more efficient and comfortable following extensive network upgrades. High speed trains (Yuksek Hizli Tren (YHT)) now operate on the Istanbul-Ankara, Ankara-Konya, and Eskisehir-Konya routes. Tickets are affordable and it's best to book online in advance, especially at peak times and during holiday periods. Tickets can be bought via the Turkish Railways

The Varda Viaduct in Adana province, known locally as Alman Köprüsü ("German Viaduct") as it was designed by German engineers in the early twentieth century.

(TCDD) ticket Web site (www.ebilet.tcddtasimacilik. gov.tr) where there is an English-language option available.

Ferries

There is a network of catamaran sea buses that offer fast and pleasant journeys between Turkey's ports, including from Istanbul to Yalova, Marmara Island, Bandırma, and more. Both passenger-only and car ferries are available on certain routes. Timetables can be viewed and tickets purchased from the official operator Web site (www.ido.com.tr), and at the catamaran stations.

LOCAL TRANSPORTATION

Buses

Turkish cities are well served by municipal buses as well as those run by private companies. There are some four hundred bus lines in Istanbul alone, most which run until midnight every night. Routes and stops are set. Your ticket (*bilet*) can be bought in advance at kiosks in bus terminals and shops, though most cities now operate an electronic pass that need to be preloaded with credit for journeys. The travel pass for Istanbul is called the Istanbulkart and can be purchased at ticket machines at stations and stops as well as some kiosks, and can be used on buses, metro, trams, and city ferry lines. Journeys made using Istanbulkart are charged less than for individual tickets, so it offers good value for money. The situation in other major cities is similar. Due to Covid-19, at the time of writing, electronic passes must be linked to your track and trace code. Smartphone apps like Moovit and Google Maps can be used for route planning around Turkey.

You'll soon find out that bus drivers in Turkey tend to drive fast and brake quickly. Always try to sit; if this is not possible, stand where you can brace yourself. There is usually no standing allowed on the shuttle buses which run from airports to city centers. These are often the cheapest and simplest option for city transfers upon arrival.

Minibuses

Private minibuses are licensed by the local authority and operate on set routes. The difference between a bus and minibus is that the minibus does not have defined stops, only a set route, and you can hop on and off where you like along the route. The first time you ride a minibus you may wonder what is going on when everyone behind you keeps saying something and then passing money up to you, to the front. They are paying their fares! Your change will come back to you from the driver in the same way.

When you want to get off, say, so that the driver can hear you, "*İnecek var*" ("I want to get off").

Dolmuş

A *dolmuş* is a special shared taxi. It has a fixed route, generally shorter than the minibus, and departs when it is full. It is a little more expensive than a minibus but usually quicker. You can use the same phrase as above

Dolmuş taxis waiting for passengers.

when you want to get out. (Try not to confuse it with "*İnek var*" which means "There is a cow"!)

Local Ferries

The ferry is a common way of crossing the Bosporus in Istanbul, or crossing the bay in Izmir. Entry to the ferry station is via a turnstile and you can use the same city pass as for buses and metro. Once the ferry has docked and passengers have disembarked, the gate is opened and you go out onto the pier. Don't copy the experienced locals and leap across the water! Wait to use the gangplank, even though this is usually just a narrow plank of wood. Enjoy the view from the ferry in nice weather; you can have tea and *simit* (sesame-coated bread ring) or a hot *sahlep* (orchis root) drink on board.

Istanbul and Izmir also have a network of catamaran fast ferries. These run less frequently than the regular ferries, and are more expensive, but the ride is quicker, the seating more luxurious, and boarding and disembarking are definitely safer.

Taxis

All official taxis in the major cities are yellow and have a license plate beginning with the letter T. At airports at the official taxi rank you may see a more luxurious taxi that is blue, or a black minivan. These have higher fares but can take more people and luggage. In town it is best to use a hailing app like BiTaksi or Uber (the latter was banned in 2019 but was permitted to reenter the market in 2021), the taxi *durak* (stand), or to use

Passengers crossing the Bosporus on a ferry service.

a taxi called from the stand by the receptionist of the office, hotel, or restaurant where you have been. Cabs can also be hailed at the roadside, just make sure the driver turns the meter on.

Normally the passenger gets in the back. If your group is more than two people and is mixed, women go in the back and a man in front. All taxis should have a *saat* (meter). You pay by distance and by time, so the meter will tick over if you are stuck in traffic (common in big cities). It is usual to tip 10 percent, and the cost of any tolls (which are not shown on the meter).

If you know the route you'd like to take, you can tell the taxi driver; otherwise, he may choose a longer route.

Remember that face-saving is a Turkish trait—if a taxi driver is lost, he may not want to admit this and may ask a passerby. (Even if he did, he could get the wrong directions, as the passerby would not want to admit to not knowing either.) Taxi drivers love to talk.

Trams and Metro

Trams and metro systems operate in cities across Turkey. These are quick and efficient modes of transport, though networks may not cover the whole town or city, and can be paid for using your city travel pass. Children under six ride for free.

A train arrives at Istanbul's Haliç metro station via the Golden Horn Bridge.

Electric scooters are available for hire in a number of
cities around the country.

In Istanbul, the underground Marmaray train
crosses the Bosporus; in Izmir the İzban train
connects to the airport and nearby towns such as
Selçuk (for Ephesus).

Shared Bikes and Scooters
As in other cities around the world, shared bike and
electric scooter systems operate in numerous cities
around Turkey. Download the relevant app for the
scooter or bike you want to use, register, and off
you go. Electric scooters are limited to roads with
a speed limit of 50 kmph. Riders must be over
eighteen, though those over sixteen may ride with
a motorcycle permit.

WHERE TO STAY

Every town has a range of hotels and cheaper
pansiyons (guest houses or hostels). Even in the
smallest towns, hotels range from one-star to at least
three-star. Although there are walk-in rates posted,
you can try to negotiate a price. Check that the price is
inclusive (*dahil*) of tax (KDV) and breakfast (*kahvaltı*).
Airbnb operates across Turkey and deals for hotels
can be found on your favorite booking site.

In a small town, or in a lower-class hotel, check
that everything in the room works before you agree
to stay. It is normal to ask to see the room first. Four-
and five-star hotels have business facilities such as
satellite TV, meeting rooms, and Internet connection,
and are likely to have a sports and leisure center.
Remember that the minibar and calls from the room
are expensive.

You will need to show ID (normally a passport) to
check in. If you don't pay at check-in, they will keep
your ID until you check out.

HEALTH

There are some standard dos and don'ts to keeping well
during your stay in Turkey. In general, locals don't drink
the tap water, and you shouldn't either. Water in main
cities like Istanbul is treated, but mineral content is high
and water can be contaminated by old pipes. Bottled
water is always best. Those with sensitive stomachs

should avoid uncooked foods such as salads, unless you are in a home or a good quality hotel or restaurant. If you get a bad cut, you must have a tetanus shot. Watch out for hepatitis and HIV in your activities; these are present but there is little public awareness of them.

If you get sunstroke, and your blood pressure falls and you feel faint, a good remedy is the yogurt drink *ayran*, as it has a high level of salt.

Good healthcare is available in the private sector. There are private hospitals and clinics in towns and cities throughout the country, with state-of-the-art technology and many medical staff who have completed training abroad. If you are taken ill in a rural area, it would be a good idea to go to the nearest large town for treatment. Although state hospitals are improving, in smaller locations they are best avoided if possible.

The ambulance service is private, and often each hospital has its own ambulance; be aware that this can mean an ambulance team will take you to its own hospital and not necessarily to the nearest one. The emergency department is called Acil Servis. Usually if you have a foreign insurance policy you will have to pay by credit card at the hospital, keep the receipt, and claim later from your policy provider.

In big cities many foreign drugs are available, most without prescription, so you can buy them over the counter at a pharmacy (*eczane*). The pharmacist can also check your blood pressure or cholesterol level, give injections, and so on.

For an ambulance, dial 112. English-speaking

operators are not a guarantee, however. Private hospitals also have their own ambulance services where English is more likely to be spoken.

Covid-19

When Covid-19 reached Turkey in early 2020, the government introduced numerous measures to control its spread. At the time of writing, tourists need to show proof of vaccination, recovery from Covid, or a negative PCR test in order to enter the country. You are then provided a track and trace QR code accessed via the government app, called HES (Hayat Eve Sığar, or "Life Fits Home" in English).

SAFETY

Travelers who dress and behave respectably are as safe in Turkey as anywhere in the world. Violent crime is not usually random; most violent crimes are crimes of passion, or retribution for a serious affront. That said, violence has been known to erupt following football matches between rival teams.

Foreign women who have moved to Istanbul from large cities in the USA or Europe often say they feel safer walking in the street in the evenings than back home. If you are a woman traveling alone or two women late at night, it is best not to attract attention to yourself or it may be assumed that you are trying to invite male company. If you are careful, you will be fine.

Western women, particularly Americans, are often misunderstood because of their openness, and in Turkey, honest curiosity or light conversation may be interpreted as flirtation. Although mixed group activities are common at school and work, it is improper for a Turkish man to show too much interest in a woman without getting to know her through his family or social circle first. He might think that a foreign woman is open to his advances. If you feel uncomfortable, tell another Turk in the group that he is too friendly for your liking. They will know how to deal with it and will be pleased to help.

Turkish men have a justified reputation for being Casanovas, and if you go out alone with a Turk he is likely to assume that you will be open to his amorous approaches. In seaside resorts or tourist areas, some Turkish men make a living by picking up Western women and showing them the town, at the women's expense.

Things can change quickly in relation to the terrorism. It is wise to obtain up-to-date information from your government before travel and to read up on current events once you've landed. Long-term residents should register with their embassy or consulate to receive updates.

Pickpocketing can occur in tourist and market areas. Be careful if people try to distract you or follow you— they may be petty thieves after your wallet or cash. Sometimes a person may approach you to change money on the street. Decline—it is often counterfeit.

In case of an emergency, police can be reached by dialing 155.

CHAPTER EIGHT

BUSINESS BRIEFING

Turkey is a rapidly developing country with sophisticated facilities in its major towns and cities. The economy used to be based on agriculture, mining and quarrying of raw materials such as coal and marble, and simple manufacturing; today it is much more diversified. Still a major exporter of crops such as dates, figs, nuts, and citrus fruit, and raw materials such as marble, Turkey is also a world leader in the manufacture of textiles and automobiles, and has a developed service sector.

Turks are very hospitable, and your business hosts will look after you. Turkey is used to international practices, and many of the hotels, restaurants, and offices in the major cities are as good as any in the West.

Business hours are typically from 9:00 a.m. to 6:00 p.m., Monday to Friday. Shops are open late, and on Saturday and Sunday. Holiday months are July and August, and the weeks of Şeker Bayramı and Kurban Bayramı.

The Levent business disctrict in Istanbul.

The polarization of Turkey's society discussed in earlier chapters, between those with secular and those with religious and conservative values, is also evident in the business world. As such, while the advice that follows is general, it's important to be aware that companies with more conservative owners will have a different feel from those with secular owners. This runs deeper than obvious issues such as whether alcohol is drunk at business events or the attitude to hiring women who wear headscarves. It covers the whole ethos of running a business, including using Islamic banking, whether to charge customers interest, and a different definition of corporate social responsibility. Because networks and relationships are so important in Turkey, you tend to find that companies are more likely to place contracts and do business with those who share their particular set of values, whether they be religious or secular.

OFFICE ETIQUETTE AND PROTOCOL

When doing business with Turks it's important to keep in mind the key values that are applicable across all of society. For example, preserving honor and saving face, both for oneself and for the other party, are paramount. People and relationships are more important than time, and making contacts is the key to success. Networking is the foundation of business in Turkey. Many foreigners fail to realize that this is how business happens: time spent building relationships is not wasted but opens doors to future success.

The best way to build a network is to develop a relationship with someone who already has good contacts. You will then be introduced as a friend. Making this first contact will involve investing time in getting to know the other party, calling them regularly, asking how things are going for them, and generally being helpful.

A possible starting point is a trade fair. Turkey has many of these, and they are an opportunity to meet potential clients, partners, and distributors. Take advantage of social opportunities and be sure to follow up quickly and frequently with a call.

Another useful route is to join trade delegations organized by government agencies or international chambers of commerce. LinkedIn is also widely used by businesspeople in Turkey for networking, as is WhatsApp, Signal, and Telegram. Having a Turkish friend add you to a relevant group is a great way to meet like-minded people—though you may want to switch off notifications as some groups have very heavy traffic. The importance of showing respect and honor means many people will post congratulations or commiseration in response to news one person on the group has shared.

Business Cards

Business cards are still widely used, often being a way to share contact details and social media pages. Those who work for multinationals may have dual-language cards, with their title and details in Turkish on one side and in English on the reverse. When people give you their business cards, treat them with respect.

Your Turkish contact may have put an ink cross mark on the back of his or her card. This practice stems from the fact that it was common to write an amount of money on the back of a business card as a pledge. The cross cancelled it.

Business Gifts

In business, gifts are given at *bayram* (official holidays). These are normally quite smart: perhaps a monogrammed diary or desk set, or a basket of choice food or preserves.

MEETINGS

Professional occasions require punctuality. Due to the vagaries of traffic in Istanbul, however, it is acceptable to be slightly late as long as you call to say you are stuck in traffic.

A business meeting usually begins with tea and an introductory chat about the participants' health, families, and the general state of business, the economy, and the world. Ten or fifteen minutes can pass before getting down to the point of the meeting. Wait for your contact to broach the subject. In time, you will be asked in detail about your company, products, and services. Only at this point is it appropriate to start talking business.

Formal address is used. In a professional setting, a person's given name will never be used on its own. Your Turkish partners will typically add "Miss" or "Mr." to the given name, addressing you as Mr. John rather than Mr. Smith, but never John. You may refer to a Turk as Mr. Ahmet or Miss Ayşe, but it is also acceptable to say "Ahmet Bey" or "Ayşe Hanım." If you speak Turkish, use the formal *siz*, not the *sen* second-person form of the verb, even if you know the person quite well.

Protocol is important, and there is a strict hierarchy. Respect should be given to those in a senior position. The face-saving aspect of Turkish business life cannot be emphasized enough. Criticism may be seen as hostility. Never say anything negative about a senior to a junior. Don't criticize someone to or in front of their peers. If a manager wishes to correct someone it is normally more effective to do so privately than in public.

It is extremely rude to interrupt, or to correct someone when they are talking. Wait politely until they have finished, and then express your point of view. If two people start to talk at the same time they will apologize and insist the other go first.

In negotiations, determine your bottom-line figure in advance. Concessions are expected and this allows room for you to compromise. Avoid strict deadlines and threats.

BUSINESS DRESS

Dress in offices is formal, and smart suits are expected. Designer labels are popular. Women often wear trousers. Some Westernized companies allow "office

An Istanbul businessman in typical work attire.

casual" all week, or just on Fridays, but they are likely to require business dress for meetings. If in doubt, dress formally.

If you are meeting at someone's home, you may be told to dress casually. This will mean "smart casual"—such as designer label, polo-neck shirt, chinos, and proper shoes—never scruffy T-shirt, non-designer jeans, or sneakers.

CANDOR AND COOPERATION

The importance placed on saving face means that the Turkish concept of honesty may sometimes differ from your own. A person may tell a white lie about their boss to protect their honor—"Ayşe Hanım is busy on the telephone," when in fact she is late for work because of the traffic. Don't make it clear that you realize this, as this would be an affront both to Ayşe Hanım's honor and that of the person you are talking to.

This principle works both ways. Turks are unlikely to let you know if they don't believe you will be able to keep to the timetable you have promised, or if they suspect your claims are exaggerated, for fear of offending your honor. It is important to ask them if they have any questions or doubts, and to make sure they realize you will not be offended by hearing their true thoughts.

Saying "I don't know" is often deemed to be weakness. Turks are likely to give a general answer rather than say that they don't know but will find out.

This is particularly true when others are present. If you sense this is happening, save your question for someone more senior, or ask it via SMS or an e-mail, so they will have a chance to research it before replying.

Turks do not like to give bad news. In response to a question concerning the whereabouts of a promised product or report you are likely to get the reply, "It's nearly ready," even if work has only just started. If you walk out of a meeting having been told, "Leave us a sample and we will test it and place an order next month," it may mean just that, or it could mean, "This is too expensive/the wrong color/no good, but we don't want to ruin your day by telling you," and the awaited order will never materialize.

Whenever possible, return favors. Turkish culture encourages reciprocity; if someone has helped you, you should help them when they need it. Using influential contacts is routine in the business world. When choosing business partners or consultants such as lawyers or accountants, it is wise to seek out those with the widest networks.

REGULATIONS

There are three experiences that are inescapable when doing business in Turkey: bureaucracy, regulations, and red tape. Turkey follows the Swiss civil code: you are not allowed to do something unless it is specifically prescribed in law. The Turkish commercial code lays down detailed rules for all sorts of things, and the plethora of regulations issued by government ministries carry the force of law. It is vital to stay up to date and informed because regulations can change frequently.

From purchasing a car to setting up a company, detailed documentation, often countersigned by a notary, is required when making applications to the authorities. Any application is accompanied by a *dilekçe* (literally, "statement of wish"), which often has to be in a set format. Most applications require at least five passport-sized photographs so carry a good stock of these. There are also often photocopy and photographic shops nearby.

Different officials may require different sets of documents for the same task. You may have to line up six times for six different signatures at the main postal sorting office just to take delivery of a parcel. Never argue with an official, as the power to sign or not sign is in his hands. Any disagreement may result in your papers going to the bottom of the pile. The Turks have a proverb: "The one who holds the official stamp in his hand has the power of Solomon."

Some processes have been simplified and can be done using the government's online Web site www.turkiye.gov.tr. This saves time, particularly for regular tasks like paying monthly taxes, but you will still encounter bureaucracy when dealing with many aspects of business life.

WOMEN IN MANAGEMENT

Women in managerial positions are well accepted. Male visitors should be polite and respectful, avoid excessive

Turkish businesswoman, entrepreneur, and e-commerce pioneer, Hanzade Doğan Boyner.

eye contact, and shake hands only if the woman offers hers first. Physical contact may not be acceptable if she is strictly religious.

LEADERSHIP AND DECISION-MAKING

Traditionally, Turkish companies operated "top down." The old-style Turkish boss is formal, and does little but give orders. Middle management is there to check and put a stamp on paperwork.

They may be members of the owner's family, and tend not to get their hands dirty.

Many companies are now changing to modern leadership techniques. Books by Western management gurus sell like hot cakes, and conferences are packed. However, the old style lingers on in public institutions, in some older managers, and in the reactive, accepting behavior of Turkish employees.

To avoid confrontation, Turks will react in the way that causes minimal embarrassment. Employees or colleagues may not give their opinion if they think you may not like it, or if you are senior to them and pointing something out could cause you to lose face. A foreign manager may struggle to get truthful feedback from junior staff. You may ask a colleague to telephone someone whom she knows to be away, but as you have asked her to do it she will not correct you in public and will make the unnecessary call.

PRESENTATION AND LISTENING STYLES

A workshop or training seminar tends to be a serious and formal affair. In general, Turks tend to think that the longer it takes, the better it is.

Formal presentations may be read and are usually impersonal. Generally, Turks use fewer jokes or "gimmicks" in a speech than Western speakers, and rarely use examples that show themselves or a colleague in a poor light. Juniors are expected to listen to their seniors and never interrupt.

TEAMWORK AND MANAGEMENT

Go slow! As part of a team, allow time for people to trust you before suggesting change. Take care to listen to everyone and to respect their ideas. Don't ever dismiss an idea in public—if you do, the person who ventured it will never suggest another idea to you again for fear of losing face.

Ultimately, the boss is the boss; the manager has clear authority to make the final decision, and the team will swing in behind him, even if they don't agree with it. People are more concerned with group success and keeping the group together than appearing to be the individual shining star. This has its pros and cons. If a problem occurs, it is difficult to get anyone to take responsibility. If you criticize decisions and don't seem to be taking part, you break the group ethos.

CONTRACTS

While trust is essential when doing business in Turkey, the contract is king. Contracts are written in Turkish, so a translator may be required.

Foreign companies should expect to encounter massive bureaucracy. You will need patience, and the services of a Turkish lawyer and accountant as there are many seemingly unpredictable decisions made at local government level, and frequent changes in the legal and regulatory environment.

Because personal relationships matter, time and patience are needed even after signature, as it is necessary to keep the other side on board with frequent contact. In the event of a dispute, try to resolve matters through a mediator and avoid going to court, which can be a very drawn-out process. If you should find yourself in court, your contract will be key in determining the verdict.

CORRUPTION

Corruption, both grand and petty, is still a problem in Turkey, although it is decreasing. Piracy and violation of intellectual property rights is also a major problem. On Transparency International's Corruption Perception Index, in 2021 Turkey ranked 96 out of 180 countries. The government's anti-corruption strategy has led to a number of public officials being dismissed.

CHAPTER NINE

COMMUNICATING

TURKS AND FOREIGN LANGUAGES

Well-educated Turks will be fluent in English, often speaking it more grammatically correctly than native speakers. Some will have been educated exclusively in English. Others may be fluent in German or French.

Turks are patient and considerate; in a group they will make sure that you are not left out, which may extend to nominating one of the group to act as your translator.

TURKISH PRONUNCIATION

Turkish words are pronounced just as they would be in English, with the following exceptions:

ı said as the "o" in woman
ç said as the "ch" in church
c said as the "j" in jam

ö said as the "eu" in the French *veut*

ş said as the "sh" in wish

ğ said as the "y" in yellow and lengthens the preceding vowel

ü said as the "u" in the French rue

Consonants are never run together.

BODY LANGUAGE

Turks are generally very emotional and tactile. However, don't miss the key point: opposite sexes tend not to touch, but with the same sex Turks are more physical than Westerners. It is considered natural and proper for two men to greet each other with a kiss on each cheek. Also, people of the same sex will walk together linking arms or holding hands without any sexual connotation involved. Friendships are carefully fostered and maintained, and physical touch is an expression of respect. People stand and sit closer than many Westerners may find comfortable. The following is a list of the most important physical gestures to be aware of while in Turkey.

GESTURES AND TABOOS

- Turks say "no" with a simple "tsk" sound, or by raising their eyebrows, or by doing both, or by doing both and throwing their head up. Each is more emphatic than the last!

- A nod of the head means "yes."
- A shake of the head means "I am not sure" (so if you do this a salesman will keep on with his patter to try to help you reach a decision).
- To say "I don't know," shrug your shoulders.
- A shrug of the shoulders with raised hands, palms upward, expresses the feeling, "What can I do about it?"
- To express to the cook or chef that a meal or dish was delicious, put the tip of your thumb to the tips of your fingers (palm up) and bounce your hand up and down.

A statue of women in conversation in Eskisehir, northwestern Turkey.

- To refuse something (such as food) politely, put your palm flat on your chest to indicate "No, thank you."
- On the first transaction of the day, a shopkeeper may scrape a coin on his chin; this means "May God bless and multiply this."
- A brush of the hands together indicates the job is finished.
- If Turks don't like someone or something, they shake their collar.
- When giving a warning to children, they wag their index finger and say, "*seni seni . . .*" ("you, you," meaning "naughty thing!")

- Children are summoned with the motion of an outstretched hand with palm down and bending the fingers forward and backward while saying, "*gel gel*" ("come, come").
- When Turks rub their index fingers together side by side, they mean, "Are you girlfriend and boyfriend?"
- When they think someone is exaggerating, they rotate their hand with palm up while saying "oh, oh, oh," meaning that they find it hard to believe what they hear.
- It is rude to show the soles of one's feet and to sit with legs crossed. Also, blowing one's nose in public is offensive. Too firm a handshake is considered impolite.

PHONES AND SIM CARDS

Landlines in Turkey are provided by Türk Telekom, but many Turks now don't even have a landline, preferring to have a cell phone, and making most of their calls using a monthly data package.

Major cities and most of the rest of the country are extremely well covered by GSM operators. Turkey uses the European system, and an American phone will not work in Turkey unless it is multiband.

You can buy a *hazır kart* (or prepaid SIM card) to put in your own cell phone for a Turkish telephone number—this will be cheaper than using your international number if you are staying for a long time. The major providers are Türkcell and Vodaphone; both have stands in the arrival halls at airports and a nationwide network of shops.

If you are staying in Turkey for more than four months, you will need to buy a phone locally as your foreign phone will only work for 120 days, unless you pay the high fee required to register it.

It is not necessarily thought rude to have your phone on during a meeting, or during a meal at a restaurant.

Pay phones are extremely hard to find and hotel charges for phone calls are high.

Normally you dial 00 for an international dial tone, before the country code. For a national code to a different city, dial 0 and then the city code. This also applies to calls in Istanbul from one side of the Bosporus to the other. Cell phone numbers start 05. You need to dial the city code (for a landline) or cell operator code if calling from a cellphone.

MAIL

Regular mail is not so reliable. Mail letters at the post office rather than in one of the few public mailboxes, as these are not always regularly emptied.

When addressing an envelope, put your details on the top left after the word Gönderen, meaning "sender." If you are sending a letter within Turkey, the envelope should be addressed in this order: name, neighborhood, street followed by apartment name and number and door number, and lastly city. A village address can be looser—terms such as "behind the mosque" may be used.

Mail can be slow or can go astray; to guarantee that a letter reaches its destination send it by registered mail.

Private cargo companies can provide twenty-four-hour delivery anywhere in the country, and are more reliable. Major companies are Aras, MNG, and Yurtiçi and they have branches in most city neighborhoods.

For both cargo and mail, local addresses are written as follows: name, neighborhood, street followed by apartment name, number, and door number, followed by city, which should be capitalized and underlined.

The following is an example:

Name
Erenköy Mah, (neighborhood)
Antalya Sok. (street)
Huzur Ap.No. 22. D.4, (apartment name and number, followed by door number)
<u>*ISTANBUL*</u> (city, underlined and in capitals)

INTERNET AND SOCIAL MEDIA

Throughout Turkey Wi-Fi access is common in cafés, restaurants, hotels, and public transport. The connection and speed may vary, but you'll most likely have access to service.

In 2022, around 80 percent of Turkey's population used the Internet on a daily basis, while around 75 percent were active social media users—an increase of 11 percent on the previous year. The most popular social media platforms in Turkey are YouTube, Instagram, Facebook, Twitter, Pinterest, and LinkedIn, followed by TikTok, Snapchat, and Twitch.

As elsewhere, posting hate speech and supporting terrorism online are crimes; in Turkey, criticizing the government can also get you into trouble. From time to time services may be disrupted, or certain sites may be taken down by order of a court. At times of crisis, or terror threats, the government may block the Internet.

TELEVISION

The TV set is a major feature of any Turkish home. In some family homes, and in many shops and restaurants, it is on all the time.

There are state channels and private channels, satellite providers like Digiturk, D-smart, and TVbu, and numerous streaming services that offer a variety of programming: news, documentaries, music, entertainment, education, soaps, and movies. Some show locally produced programs, including Turkish versions of CNN and Fox. Others broadcast foreign programs and films dubbed into Turkish. Some channels make a point of showing foreign films or serials in the original language, with subtitles.

Don't be surprised to see a circle on the screen blacking out a cigarette or a glass of wine in your favorite foreign film or show—it is illegal for television channels in Turkey to show these.

NEWSPAPERS

Newspapers are widely read, though there has been a decline in print production in recent years, as people increasingly turn to digital media. According to 2021 statistics, there were 2,164 newspapers published nationwide in 2020, down from 2,337 the previous year. The four national papers with the widest circulation are *Sabah*, *Sözcü*, *Hürriyet*, and *Posta*. English national newspapers include *The Hurriyet Daily News* and *Daily Sabah*, with editorial policies representing different aspects of the Turkish social spectrum. These can be read online for free.

CONCLUSION

Despite the societal changes that have taken place in Turkey in recent decades, and that continue to take place, old-time values hold strong across society: respect for elders and authority, loyalty to and reliance upon the group, in particular the family, setting great store on personal relationships, and the importance of honor and saving face. The Turks you will meet will all identify with somewhere on the spectrum of modern Turkish society, and this will dictate how they go about their daily lives. Whether avowedly secular or religious conservative, however, you will find your Turkish friends to be very group and people oriented, loyal, sociable, and very hospitable. As a foreign guest you will be warmly welcomed, and will find help to be offered readily, should you need.

After spending time in Turkey, some local traits may strike you as contrary. You will notice that many drive aggressively and always seem to be in a hurry, while at the same time lack punctuality and often show up late for appointments. Many have a strong dislike for rules and regulations, and yet the red tape in official transactions can border on the absurd. Of course, most newcomers will suffer the handicap of not understanding the language and, by viewing Turkey through foreign eyes, can fall easily into making wrong assumptions. Instead, allow this unique and important country to show you a different way of looking at the world. In this book we hope to have eased your path into this complex, rich, and fascinating society.

USEFUL APPS

Communication and Socializing

Concerts and events: Biletix

Dictionary: SesliSözlük

Learn Turkish: Wilingua, Babbel

Property to rent: Sahibinden

Translation: Google (although it can do a poor job with word-endings).

Travel and Transportation

Electric scooter hire: Providers vary from city to city.

Government track and trace app: HayatEveSığar (HES). The app is called Life Fits Home in English.

Accomodation: Otelz.com, Booking.com, Airbnb.

Navigation and route planning: GoogleMaps and Yandex are most widely used. Most cities have their own routeplaning apps. Istanbul's is Mobiett.

Intercity buses: Each company has its own app where you can view timetables and book tickets. Bilet.com is a good general site.

City transport: Each city has its own transport card for use on local buses, trains, etc. Use the app for top-ups, etc. For Istanbul: Istanbulkart, Ankara: Ankarakart, Izmir: Izkart.

Ride hailing: BiTaksi is market leader.

Shared bicycles: Some cities have this. For Istanbul: Isbike.

Trains: Tcdd

Food and Shopping

Fashion: Trendyol, n11. Many stores also have their own app.

Flowers and gift delivery: ÇiçekSepeti

General retail: HepsiBurada, GittiGidiyor

Grocery delivery: Migros, HepsiDirect, Getir

Restaurant food delivery: YemekSepeti

FURTHER READING

Atatürk: The Birth of a Nation. Istanbul: Ministry of Culture of the Republic of Turkey/Revak, 1998.

Baer, Marc David. *The Ottomans: Khans, Caesars, and Caliphs*. Basic Books, 2021.

De Busbecq, Ogier. *Turkish Letters*. Oxford: Oxford University Press, 2001.

Eyuboğlu, Hughette. *From the Steeple to the Minaret: Living Under the Shadow of Two Cultures*. Istanbul: Çitlembik Publishers, 2004.

Finkel, Caroline. *Osman's Dream: The Story of the Ottoman Empire*. New York: Basic Books, 2006.

Freely, John. *Inside the Seraglio: Private Lives of the Sultans in Istanbul*. London: Penguin, 1999.

Haldon, J.F. *Byzantium in the Seventh Century*. Melbourne: Cambridge University Press, 1990.

Kinross, Patrick. *Atatürk: The Rebirth of a Nation*. London: Phoenix Press, 2003.

Kinzer, Stephen. *Crescent and Star: Turkey Between Two Worlds*. New York: Farrar, Straus, and Giroux, 2001.

Mansel, Philip. *Constantinople: City of the World's Desire 1453–1924*. Melbourne: Cambridge University Press, 1995.

Öktem, Kerem. *Angry Nation: Turkey Since 1989*. London: Zed Books, 2011.

Özdemir, Adil, and Kenneth Frank. *Visible Islam in Modern Turkey*. London: Macmillan Press Limited, 2000.

Pamuk, Orhan. *Istanbul: Memories and the City*. London: Faber & Faber, 2006.

Pope, Hugh and Nicole. *Turkey Unveiled: A History of Modern Turkey*. New York: The Overlook Press, 2004.

Runciman, Steven. *A History of the Crusades, Vol.1–3*. London: Penguin, 1990.

Scott, Alev. *Turkish Awakening*. Faber & Faber, 2014.

Seal, Jeremy. *A Coup in Turkey*. Chatto & Windus, 2021.

Stone, Norman. *Turkey: A Short History*. Thames & Hudson, 2014

In-Flight Turkish. New York: Living Language, 2001.

PICTURE CREDITS

INDEX